THE FORGOTTEN
DESERT
MOTHERS

SECOND EDITION

Sayings, Lives, and Stories of Early Christian Women

LAURA SWAN

Paulist Press
New York/Mahwah, NJ

Grateful acknowledgment is made for the use of the following excerpts: Adapted from *The Life of Blessed Syncletica* by Pseudo-Athanasius, translated by Elizabeth Bryson Bongie. Copyright © 1995 by Elizabeth Bryson Bongie. Reprinted by permission of Peregrina Publishing. Adapted from *The Sayings of the Desert Fathers*, translated by Benedicta Ward. Copyright © 1975 by Benedicta Ward. Reprinted by permission of Cistercian Publications.

Cover image: *Eight Righteous Women*, used by permission of Holy Transfiguration Monastery, Brookline, MA.
Cover design by Cheryl Finbow
Book design by Lynn Else

Library of Congress Cataloging-in-Publication Data
Names: Swan, Laura, 1954– author.
Title: The forgotten Desert Mothers : sayings, lives, and stories of early Christian women / Laura Swan.
Description: Second edition. | New York / Mahwah, NJ : Paulist Press, [2022] | Includes bibliographical references and index. | Summary: "An introduction to the sayings, lives, stories, and spirituality of women in the postbiblical, early Christian movement"—Provided by publisher.
Identifiers: LCCN 2021042815 (print) | LCCN 2021042816 (ebook) | ISBN 9780809155903 (paperback) | ISBN 9781587689932 (ebook)
Subjects: LCSH: Monastic and religious life of women—History—Early church, ca. 30–600.
Classification: LCC BR195.M65 S93 2022 (print) | LCC BR195.M65 (ebook) | DDC 270.2082—dc23
LC record available at https://lccn.loc.gov/2021042815
LC ebook record available at https://lccn.loc.gov/2021042816

ISBN 978-0-8091-5590-3 (paperback)
ISBN 978-1-58768-993-2 (e-book)

Published by Paulist Press
997 Macarthur Boulevard
Mahwah, New Jersey 07430
www.paulistpress.com

Printed and bound in the
United States of America

CONTENTS

Cover Icon: *Eight Righteous Women*, written by a monk of Holy Transfiguration Monastery, Brookline, Massachusetts.

Back Row (L–R)

Saint Photini: The name given by the Eastern Orthodox tradition to the Samaritan woman who encountered Jesus at the well, as told in John 4:1–30. Tradition teaches that she was later martyred.

Saint Melania of Rome (see chapter 6)

Saint Eudoxia Samaritan: A prostitute who converted to Christianity and was martyred

Saint Pelagia the Penitent (see chapter 7)

Front Row (L–R)

Macrina (see chapter 6)

Mary the Egyptian (see chapter 7)

Mary Magdalene: Close friend and companion of Jesus as well as the first witness of the resurrection (Luke 24 and John 20)

Maria of Mesopotamia (see chapter 7)

PREFACE

When I was pursuing graduate studies in theology, I found much of my own religious understanding to be deeply challenged. My studies continually called me to reflect upon my own life experience and understanding of God as the starting place for doing theology. As a strong thinker and avid reader, I had presumed that good theology was strictly rational: if my thinking was clear and I conformed my behavior to rational thought, I would be on the right track.

During my graduate studies I witnessed death, suicide, and changing relationships. I felt a growing awareness of a call to the monastic life. All of this caused me to question my understanding of life and how it *should* be. Transition came upon transition, waves swept over and carried me forward. In this journey, I found myself clarifying values and making choices that moved me inward and closer to God.

I came to know the desert intimately, and all its painful stripping and intense silence. With time, as I learned to listen deep within, what had seemed barren was transformed into abundant simplicity. The deafening silence and the apparent absence of God revealed the idols I held dear. God yearned to strip away all my false gods so that I might encounter the authentic I AM.[1] My interior journey was toward inner simplicity…toward fertile soil from whence my truest self might emerge.

I was hardly prepared for the inner revolution that would result when I began to confront the possibility that my own experience had value and meaning. Absolutes crashed down, certitudes faltered, and I questioned everything I believed. I began to discover my inner voice, to listen to my own values, desires, and passions. I was invited to listen to my feelings, emotions, and inner stirrings for the wisdom they contain. I discovered the freedom to stop hauling around the dead wood that had burdened me, the *shoulds* and the *oughts*, the quiet tyrant within that tells me I am not good enough. I was beginning to discover that God's simple abundance *is* truly abundant.

During this season of transition and inner turmoil, I was introduced to the voices of people from nondominant cultures and differing experiences. I was challenged to stretch my thinking and to recognize the ways in which I am both oppressor and oppressed. I learned to notice those whose voices and life experiences were missing as I read theology and church history.

It was during my period of initial formation in my monastery that I first encountered the desert ascetics. The stark imagery in the stories of these urban and desert dwellers who sought fiery, passionate relationships with God captured me. Unfortunately, with rare exception, the stories were about men. I grew increasingly frustrated with the lack of information on the women who had also dwelt in the desert.

I began to pursue and collect traces of these women's stories. It often felt like the sleuthing work of Sister Frevisse or Brother Cadfael in the medieval whodunits I enjoy. I found myself tracking down clues, following strands of evidence, and reading the shadows of texts to find these women. Clues often took the form of rare scholarly material, frequently in footnotes and asides.

Women's history has often been relegated to the shadow world: felt but not seen. Many of our church *fathers* became prominent because of *women*. Many of these fathers were educated and supported by strong women, and some are even credited with founding movements that were actually begun by the women in their lives.

Early church histories frequently make brief mention of women dwelling in the desert, living as urban solitaries, or residing in or near monastic communities; yet it is the stories of the men that are preserved and told.

Ancient Christian hagiography can be difficult and heavy reading, even for the most courageous souls. Its writers were more concerned with capturing the heart and essence of the person rather than with historical fact. The stories were written to teach moral concepts and to encourage the hearer. Detailed accounts helped the biographer to highlight teachings, honor the saint, and make the story worth hearing. To assist our twenty-first-century hearts and sensibilities, I retell many of these stories, cutting out the most heavy-handed elaboration. Where it is helpful or interesting, I include translated excerpts from the original texts to allow the ancient storytellers to be heard.

The Forgotten Desert Mothers: Sayings, Lives, and Stories of Early Christian Women was conceived, nurtured, and matured in community. Members of my monastic community introduced me to some of the forgotten voices of the early Christian movement and encouraged me on my pursuit of the many shadow voices that were lurking, waiting to be heard.

I live in the most ideal situation for a writer. I dwell in the midst of creative souls who encourage others to pursue their own visions, dreams, and passions. I am among women who know beyond any shadow of doubt that women are created fully and completely in the image and likeness of God. I have discovered that such a strong feminine atmosphere affirms and nurtures the gifts of men as well as those of women. I am privileged with interaction among retreatants, guests, and audiences whose questions keep me probing and searching. Their energy and exuberance for life—and for the things of God—keep me on the quest.

◆ ◆ ◆

In the twenty years since the publication of *The Forgotten Desert Mothers*, I have been deeply moved by the response of readers around the world. A deep hunger was tapped. Women yearned to know more of their heritage as women within the Christian tradition and discovered a significant thread of this sacred story. Men also were delighted with a more balanced view of early Christianity. The number of languages *The Forgotten Desert Mothers* has been translated into surprised and delighted me.

Scholars continue their explorations of this movement into the desert and the literature that resulted. Archeologists have been unearthing sites of early desert dwellers and their small monastic communities, indicating that many of these sites were clearly occupied by women. The sheer number of tombstones discovered around the greater Mediterranean world speaks to the recognized leadership roles held by women. Women monastics had already established the tradition of educating children in nearby villages. Scholars have been increasingly willing to acknowledge that ammas and monastic mothers were a significant influence in the early Christian movement, even though many of their writings, their voice, have been lost to history.

The ammas still call to us today. Contemporary scholars have been unpacking a sophisticated theology from the *sayings* and *lives* of the desert ammas, such as their teachings on humility. Given our growing ecological crisis, contemporary theologian Douglas Christie built upon his earlier work on the desert ascetics and their wisdom teachings to present a case for a "contemplative ecology," a particular way of thinking about and engaging ecological concerns that is rooted in a distinctive form of contemplative spiritual practice. He reminds us that the desert ascetics were deeply connected to creation as God's cathedral.

Preface

I am grateful for all the ongoing meticulous work of scholars seeking to build a more balanced perspective of early Christianity, generously sharing their pursuits with others.

Laura Swan, OSB
Lacey, Washington

Timeline of the Forgotten Desert Mothers

200   250   300   350   400   450   500   550   600

235 Juliana

270–304 Menodora
Metrodora
Nymphodora
Manna

312–324 Romana
d. 340 Macrina the Elder
327–380 Macrina the Younger
325–410 Marcella
Asella
342–411 Melania the Elder
347–404 Paula the Elder
d. 418 Eustochium
365–410 Olympias, Deaconess
d. 390 Vitalina
d. 399 Fabiola
369–400 Photina
380–434 Melania the Younger
380–c. 460 Amma Syncletica
397–   Paula the Younger
Matrona of Perge
410–   Euphrosyne of Alexandria
420–480 Cerona
424–520 Matrona
c. 440–500 Elisabeth the Wonderworker
450–530 Mary the Pilgrim, Euphemia
c. 470–556 Caesaria the Patrician
c. 500–550 Maria the Harp Player
c. 500–580 Shirin
c. 520–575 Anastasia the Patrician
c. 550–   Sosiana
c. 570–   Athanasia

Chapter One

THE WORLD OF
THE DESERT MOTHERS

Christianity is a living, emerging, and growing religious movement. Every generation and every culture engages with and interprets the core message and person of Jesus of Nazareth: *We are not stepchildren; we are all born of God!* As the Jesus movement spread throughout the provinces of the Roman Empire, every individual and every community wrestled with the meaning this message had for their lives. Diverse expressions—rooted in the gospel message—emerged. The ebbs and flows of growth and renewal, along with individual geniuses who inspired others to the new way of life, supported this diversity. Differing forms of the eremitic and monastic lifestyles emerged side by side. The developments were amorphous and varied.

Christianity was initially a home-centered faith. The destruction of the temple in 70 CE, the Diaspora of the Jewish community, and the experience of increasing alienation from mainstream culture resulted in domestic dwellings becoming the places for community meetings.[1] Local believers gathered in homes for the Lord's Supper, for baptism, for worship, and for meetings. There was no ordained priesthood as we understand it today. Women presided over their homes, a sphere of authority men would have recognized and honored. Given that the Eucharist, in part, evolved from the Seder, women often would have overseen the breaking of the bread. Sharing in the life, death, and resurrection of Jesus was deeply experiential. Discussion about this most central celebration of belief came later, evolved in systemized fashion, and is called *theology*.

The early believers were concerned with the imminent return of Christ, and with seeking and preparing converts for this longed-for day. The early baptismal statement quoted by Saint Paul in his letter to the Galatians: "There is no such thing as Jew and Greek, slave and free, male and female—for all are one in Christ,"[2] deeply shaped the minds of the first followers of the Way. Success varied, especially when there were clashes over authority, leadership, cultural differences, and the understanding of the nature and role of women and slaves. Although never lived out perfectly, oneness in Christ was a deeply held value.

Both women and men were involved in evangelization and works of mercy to the poor, orphans, and prisoners. Women held leadership positions: Ancient tombstones reveal a history of women bearing titles such as *ruler of the synagogue, deacon, presbyter,* and *honorable woman bishop*.[3] Yet there were struggles in these attempts at integration. Women and slaves shared in the work of evangelization, catechesis, and the building of faith communities. Some of these faith communities were culturally Jewish, others Greek or Roman. Some emphasized the prophetic gifts.

In the fourth century, Christianity gained acceptance and became the official religion of the Roman Empire. With this transition, leadership within the Christian movement became increasingly public. Social mores required that women remain in the home and out of the public sphere. Despite Galatians 3:28, pressure began to build for women to be removed from public leadership in conformity with custom.[4]

In spite of this, the believing community was lively and accepting. Women were in positions of leadership: preaching,

teaching, and living as ascetics. The church was not yet organized as it is today. Leaders were called forth from the community to serve as teachers, preachers, and in prophetic roles.
Prophetic utterances and charismatic healing gifts abounded.
Some bishops supported women as prophets and ascetics,
while others tried to control and minimize their influence.
The prophetic role tended to be outside the increasingly reg-
ulated life of the church. It was much easier for bishops to
monitor and influence teachers than those who claimed to be
prophets speaking in the name of God.

SOCIAL AND POLITICAL INFLUENCES

The marginalization of Christianity resulted from societal resistance and persecution by the Roman Empire. Women
were deeply attracted to the Christian movement, in which
they could exercise freedom they did not have in the dominant
culture. These were among the numerous factors that affected
the development of the eremitic and cenobitic monastic traditions.

Persecution, martyrdom, and a deep desire for meaning
fueled Christians' ardent passion and their willingness to pay
a high price to follow Christ. This influenced their spirituality, their search for a challenging and personally fulfilling
spiritual journey. They followed the Jewish custom of praying
several times a day, and some began to pursue intense lives of
prayer. Fasting, voluntary poverty, deprivations, silence, and
deep prayer became a way of living a continuous martyrdom
once the persecutions ended.

The desire to be like Christ and to live as one in Christ led
to experimentation in community living. Some lived in solitude on their family estates or rented small rooms on the edge
of their villages. Others began to live together in small groups,
frequently in the homes of the wealthy, whose dwellings were

usually made up of a series of buildings that could easily accommodate followers and the inevitable guests. Although prayers were shared in a dedicated sacred space within a complex, most urban monastics frequented local churches as well. Customs began to emerge among ascetics and loosely formed monastic communities. Along with reflections on the gospel, these customs developed into rules, which in turn became guides for their common life. A monastic and ascetic culture began to emerge.

Christian monasticism began in the home. The first communities usually included relatives, dependents, and household slaves.[5] This inclusiveness had a deep impact upon monastic and desert spirituality. Life was centered around times of communal prayer, private prayer, services in local churches, the study of scripture and the writings of the leaders of the movement, and service to the poor. Some experienced a call to move away from the common life toward solitude.

Although monastic communities and solitaries could be found in most cities of the empire, a movement began toward small villages and the desert. Urban Christianity tended to be composed of the middle and upper classes—households often became Christian at the lead of the matriarch and/or patriarch—but desert ascetics and community members were a mixture of unlettered, rural peasants and the urban educated. Evidence indicates that those who were uneducated when they entered were encouraged to memorize the psalms and other scriptures, and even to learn to read themselves. Rural ascetics preferred a slower and quieter life in the small towns and deserts they were familiar with. Urban ascetics were drawn to the desert for privacy and quiet.

Factors that influenced this movement to the countryside included epidemics, political corruption, social instability including crime, restrictive laws, heavy taxation by the Roman government, persecutions, and later the theological debates within Christianity. Many disciples experienced a conflict between the growing power associated with the institutionalization of the church and the pursuit of holiness. Christianity's move from the margins of society and from the home to the dominant strata of society and the public basilicas left some believers feeling that Christianity was compromised. Some felt that the church was in danger of losing its prophetic character and of becoming secularized, and that convenience and political expedience motivated some conversions.

As Christianity moved into the mainstream, the movement toward the desert and the monastic life increased. Many women had found in Christianity a freedom that enabled them to break with their culture and exercise leadership that they could not in Roman society. In a home-centered, marginal movement, women could preside at meetings in their homes and serve as evangelists, apostles, and teachers.

Unfortunately, women who had played significant roles in the ministry and leadership of Christianity found their participation dwindling as Christianity merged with the larger society and its male leaders grew increasingly uncomfortable with women in public roles. As leadership opportunities within mainstream Christianity decreased, the desert and the monastery offered women a greater sense of physical and spiritual autonomy.

The movement toward the desert and the monastery occurred at several different levels. As ascetics physically moved away from Roman society, they also began to disengage from its culture. Trappings that revealed their social class, such as fine clothing, jewelry, and hairstyles, were dropped in favor of the common and simple. The ascetics sought to "disappear" by becoming one with other seekers.

The ascetics[6] favored dark or natural colored clothing like that of the poor, and they concealed or cropped their hair. Women favored monastic garb with generous hoods to cover themselves in public and frequently chose to dress as males. They sought to minimize their sexuality as part of their ascetic practice, wanting to become like the angels. This was also practical: they were less apt to be bothered by others, especially robbers, if they appeared to be eunuchs.

In contrast to our notions of hygiene, the ascetics also refrained from bathing. The early Christians disapproved of the custom of bathing for several reasons. It was a public activity, and the public baths sometimes mixed the genders. Many Christians associated the public baths with lewd behavior, inappropriate for believers. Some felt that it was inappropriate to see someone else's nude body. Many believed that bathing stirred sexual passions—presumed to be the demon of fornication—and would cause avoidable problems. They did daily battle against their own hormones.

ENTRANCE TO THE DESERT OR MONASTERY

Those who decided to dedicate themselves to the ascetic life sought a spiritual elder. An *amma* or *abba* was someone seasoned in the ascetic life who was known to have reached a level of maturity and wisdom and had experience in teaching by example, exhortation, story, and instruction.

The ritual of receiving the monastic garb and often the monastic tonsure occurred at the beginning of the amma/disciple relationship. The disciple usually moved into the elder's home, monastic community, or desert cell. A simple coarse mat, a sheepskin, a lamp, and vessels for water and oil were the common contents of the ascetic's home. Usually the ascetic would eat one simple, often vegetarian, meal a day. Sleep was kept to a minimum, both as an ascetical practice and to leave more time for prayer.

A deep spiritual bond formed as the amma taught—more often by example than by words. The disciple prayed as the amma prayed. The disciple worked alongside the amma, weaving baskets, rope, and cloth, and distributing alms to the poor as the amma did. Ascetics were committed to supporting themselves completely by the work of their own hands. The rejection of Roman social status included rejecting unearned wealth from the labor of slaves and servants.

As the ammas honored and valued silence, talk was kept to a minimum. The desert ammas recognized that our words reveal our heart and cautioned their followers to be wise about what they said. Their silence enabled them to receive, savor, and ponder the life-giving word.

The amma journeyed and struggled alongside her disciple but maintained the detachment necessary for discernment. Communication was open and honest. The disciple shared her heart's struggles, and the amma did not hide her own humanity. The knowledge and wisdom to deal with unruly or false passions was learned by long, hard living. These women were aware of the necessity of self-understanding and the importance of taking responsibility for one's own actions.

The desert way of amma and disciple was one of hard work, a lifetime of striving to redirect every aspect of body, mind, and inner world toward God. These ammas were "practiced in peeling back the layers of silence, pierced to the core the hearts of fellow seekers and laid bare for them the voice of the living God."[7]

The desert ammas dedicated time each day to their studies as well as to prayer. The prayerful attitude that permeated the day as well as the seven times specifically dedicated to prayer that would evolve into the Divine Office were the nourishment of their day. The Eucharist was less frequent, usually only on Sundays. Some who dwelt in complete solitude would go months and years without receiving the Eucharist.

They cultivated simplicity in their lifestyle, including simplicity in their emotions and attitudes. They sought to be mindful and intentional about their actions: they were attentive to *how* they washed clothing and utensils and *how* they spoke to one another. Mindlessness was the enemy of the inner journey.

The desert ammas cultivated solitude in order to intensify their inner journey to their goal of union with God. Solitude allowed for greater silence where they could better listen for the voice of God. Solitude could be found in the city as well as in the desert. It was not uncommon for these women to move between their monastic communities and the desert.

The cell, whether in a monastery or the desert, was important to their spirituality. The cell was the place of spiritual combat, the place where one faced one's truest self and deepened awareness of one's sin and woundedness. If the ascetic could not find God in the cell, then she would not find God elsewhere. The true ascetic remains—both then and now—within the cell in mind, body, and spirit, and perseveres there until she attains true unity with God.

Ascetics often owned books. Codices of the scriptures, especially in Coptic, the vernacular of Egypt, were copied. Secular as well as sacred writings were read.

> Books in the desert often came to be stored in churches near monasteries; undoubtedly most of these early books—and collections—were of holy Scripture or lectionaries designed for public or private reading. But they were later joined by collections of homilies, doctrinal statements such as encyclical letters from the archbishop of Alexandria or canons from the ecumenical councils, lives and sayings of the saints.[8]

Texts from early church fathers in Coptic and Greek, letters of Athanasius and others during the christological controversies, and the writings and sayings of other monastics would have been found in many monastic communities.

A later catalogue of Coptic texts from the library of the Monastery of Saint Macarius in Egypt shows numerous copies of *Lives, Martyrdoms, and Sayings* of the desert Fathers as well as other monastic writings, such as homilies. Tradition mattered to the ancient monks. What the saints of old had said and lived was worth reading about and hearing again: the saints continued to offer instruction, guidance, consolation, precepts, and edification. Theirs was holy wisdom, passed on to new generations.[9]

For example, the ascetics Juliana and Melania were noted for their large and varied collections of books.

It might seem that the desert ascetics and monastics were isolated from the local and universal church, but the contrary was true. People came for spiritual direction and counseling. Bishops often involved the ascetics in heated theological debates. Monastics and hermits—when opportunity came their way—sought to convert nonbelievers to Christianity. Some adhered to orthodox and others to heterodox positions. They understood themselves as defenders of the true faith. Surviving letters and treatises reveal people deeply concerned with the development of Christianity and theology.

THE AMMA AS PILGRIM

The ammas sought out remote geographical locations, often those with hostile environments. Chosen sites were characterized by the presence of strong winds, wild animals, lack of water and foliage, and little access to basic necessities. The desert ammas felt they were doing battle in the wilderness. The desert refined their inner strength and resolve and deepened their sense of utter dependence on God. It was a place of death—a place to die to the false self and false supports, bury old ways and attitudes—and it was the realm of the spiritual and demonic. The desert ascetics believed that close proximity to the forces of nature quickened their spirit in prayer.

The ammas went to places such as the deserts of Egypt, Syria, Persia, and present-day Turkey. They were found all around the Mediterranean world, northward into Gaul and later Ireland and Britain. Favored sites were often within a day's walk of a small village in order to maintain some contact outside the community. Caves, ruins of old buildings, family tombs, islands, coastal headlands, and the fenlands of the North were common sites. Communities of seekers might spring up around a desert elder, near a cathedral, or often on a family estate.

Desert ascetics believed that the greatest enemies of the inner journey were haste, crowds, and noise. The desert was a place for quieting the inner noise that kept them from hearing the whispers of God. In the desert, spiritual testing and transformation were expected and engaged. The lack of comforts and material distractions, and isolation from the complexity of human society led to growth in spiritual insight.

The ammas sought to draw close to heaven. To be forgotten by society was to become like the angels, and they strove to limit their contact with others to only the most necessary relationships. They considered themselves aliens awaiting the heavenly city, and removing distractions supported their desire to continuously gaze toward heaven. Unfortunately for us, they were too successful; sources for their lives and sayings are limited.

THE AMMA AND RELATIONSHIPS

Although ammas yearned for solitude, most also had relationships with others. There were colleagues, followers, and friends, some of whom were deaconesses, some who lived in monastic communities. Some ammas were themselves ordained deaconesses. Their history is also the history of the early monastic movement and the development of the diaconate.

Many ammas began their ascetic journeys in monastic communities and later moved into the desert. Some were solitaries attached to a monastic settlement. Most had significant relationships of mutual support with monastic communities. Echoes of their stories often appear in the histories of monasteries.

For other ammas, the journey was reversed. They began as solitaries who found themselves surrounded by seekers. This circle of followers would begin to form a type of monastic community, under the guidance of the amma. Individual followers might then move on to pursue a solitary life; others remained in the community. In the early years of Christianity, these communities were referred to as "communal households" or as "communities of solitaries."

Some ammas would leave these young communities to return to the desert. At times, they were successful in their quest for solitude. At other times, they were again followed into the desert by seekers. Many of the surviving stories reflect this experience.

Frequently, women connected to the Imperial family established and led monastic communities. Some were widows who wanted a life focused on God and service to others. Monastic life allowed them the freedom to do this while continuing to use their influence in politics as members of the Imperial family. Other women refused arranged marriages and used their wealth and landed estates to live as they chose. Women's monasteries were soon centers of Christian culture and learning, and bishops in newly converted regions sought out women to establish monasteries to anchor the church.

Monasticism and the ascetic movement also spread through the veneration of saints. Sites of devotion sprung up around Mary Magdalene, Genovefa (the patron of Paris), the martyr Blandina, and Martin of Tours. Believers flocked to these sites, either on pilgrimage or to live a life of devotion nearby. Solitary ascetics and small communities developed reputations for their devotion to prayer and to serving the poor and pilgrims. Often their command of scripture or their scholarly endeavors were overshadowed by the stories of their generosity.

THE LIVES AND SAYINGS

Stories of these women's lives and teachings began as oral traditions savored and shared by their followers, friends, and families. Eyewitnesses recorded some of these, others were written down after many years. Miracles attributed to the intercession of these women were included. Often these stories would be embellished in a fashion we may find unpalatable today. Writers were more concerned with convincing the reader to take a moral stance and promulgating the value of self-denial, the importance of the inner journey, and the power and efficacious nature of prayer. The kernel of the teaching was important, not historical accuracy as we understand it today.

The desert ammas who are recorded in history represent only a small fraction of the number of women who lived as ascetics. The goal of the desert dwellers was to disappear, and often they were successful. Many of the histories, writings, and teachings are lost. Most of the stories preserved revolve around wealthier, better educated women from prominent families who wanted their famous relatives to be remembered for posterity. Stories of truly poor women—not those who gave their wealth away—are the exception.

The stories of the ammas paint a portrait of colorful, powerful, loving, and generous women. They could be opinionated and at times seem harsh to our modern ears. These ammas did not allow cultural norms and expectations for women to thwart their call or limit their pursuit of God. Their lives were as prophetic as their rarely spoken words.

The ammas were passionate and single-hearted in their desert journey. They spoke frankly, openly, and boldly: to disciples and pilgrims, to church and secular leaders. They listened to and proclaimed the signs of their times. They were gifted and committed to their call. Generous, self-giving, and liberated, the desert mothers were determined and intentional about their journey toward God. They were courageous, purposeful, prayerful, single-minded, discerning, and responsive to the needs of those around them. They lived the gospel call, seeking to incarnate God's presence in their midst.

These Lives advertise their mobility, independence, and empowerment. They reveal the context of the desert movement and provide insight into the early development of Christianity. These women were fiercely independent, with inner strength and determination that enabled them to go against cultural expectations and pursue their chosen lifestyles. Sometimes their family ties would be a hindrance, at other times a great benefit. These women were often leaders and shapers of the Christian movement. An informal network among desert dwellers and monastics continually expanded over the years due to the desert dwellers' reputation as wisdom figures and their radical interpretation of the gospel message.

Chapter Two

DESERT SPIRITUALITY

Amma Syncletica said:

"Whatever we do or gain in this world, let us consider it insignificant in comparison to the eternal wealth that is to come. We are on this earth as if in a second maternal womb. In that inner recess we did not have a life such as we have here, for we did not have there solid nourishment such as we enjoy now, nor were we able to be active as we are here, and we existed without the light of the sun and of any glimmer of light. Just as, then, when we were in that inner chamber, we did without many of the things of this world, so also in the present world we are impoverished in comparison with the kingdom of heaven. We have sampled the nourishment here; let us reach for the Divine! We have enjoyed the light in this world; let us long for the sun of righteousness! Let us regard the heavenly Jerusalem as our homeland....Let us live prudently in this world that we may obtain eternal life."[1]

Desert spirituality is characterized by the pursuit of abundant simplicity—simplicity grounded in the possession of little— and the abundance of God's presence. Yearning for complete union with God, desert ascetics sought to remove all obstacles to the deepening of this relationship. Obstacles included unhelpful attitudes and motives, thoughts that stalled their pursuit of God, and emotional ties that complicated their inner journeys.

The desert ascetics' relationships were nonpossessive: They cared for others while leaving them free. Concern for reputation was discarded. Feelings were acknowledged and listened to for their wisdom but were subjected to the discipline of the heart's goal to seek God. Through self-mortification, the desert ascetics sought to control disordered passions that distracted them from their deepening relationship with God so that they could actively cultivate a burning love for God.

Although the journey began with giving away possessions, desert ascetics understood that what possessed them was greater than the sum of goods owned. All that owned them, all that possessed their minds and hearts, their attachments and compulsions, must be reconciled and healed. Desert ascetics called this process of moving toward inner freedom *detachment*. Detachment allows for greater direct experience of the Divine Presence as the seeker is freed from distractions.

Desert ascetics understood that the cultivation of inner freedom was vital to deepening their experience of God. As they deepened their interior freedom, all aspects of their *false self* was removed and a clearer understanding of their *truest self* emerged.[2] It is this true self that dwells deeply with God. In the abundant simplicity of our true self, we experience deepest joy.

Desert spirituality was expressed in compassion: tender love and deep, practical care for the poor and dispossessed. It was a spiritual stance of quiet acceptance of all persons who came to the door—each was received as Christ. The ammas understood that compassion and tender love cultivated a healthy humility. Desert spirituality was nonconformist: Ammas passed on their living example, but where or how a disciple carried on the desert tradition was open to a myriad of possibilities. It was the quality of the inner journey that mattered.

Desert spirituality was deeply intimate and vulnerable. It was taught one on one. To hide one's faults from one's amma was to defeat the inner journey. The amma met with the pilgrim privately, and the words given were personal. The aim was an honest and intimate relationship with the Beloved. The stripping inherent to the desert journey required and deepened the capacity for vulnerability.

Desert spirituality was incarnational, in the sense that Christ was understood to dwell within the soul of each person. This understanding had deep impact on their care for the poor—each encounter with another was a meeting with God. This was not incarnational spirituality as we understand it today. The desert ascetics tended to be suspicious of the human body and its contradictory feelings, emotions, drives, and passions. They understood *self* as completed or made whole solely in God.

ASCETICISM

Amma Syncletica said:
"Just as dreadful qualities are attached to one another (for example, envy follows upon avarice, as do treachery, perjury, anger, and remembrance of wrongs), so the opposite qualities of these vices are dependent upon love. I mean, of course, gentleness and patience, as well as endurance, and the ultimate good—holy poverty. It is not possible for anyone to acquire this virtue (I mean, to be sure, love) apart from holy poverty, for the Lord did not enjoin love on one person, but on all. Those, therefore, who have resources must not overlook those who have needs. The workings of love, in fact, are not concealed."[3]

Desert spirituality developed around all practices, passed on from amma to disciple, that dispossessed the ascetic of *all* that kept her or him from God. Asceticism was valued in its ability to move the seeker toward authentic freedom. It was about reordering priorities in support of the inner journey. Anything that supported this journey was acceptable; all else was rejected as superfluous. Desert ascetics reduced their possessions to the minimum—a sleeping mat, several clay jars, books, and the clothing on their bodies. Fasting and abstinence from meat were practiced to help them become interiorly more attentive and alert to the movements of God's Spirit. Fasting to the point of bodily harm was condemned. Some ascetics ignored this condemnation, fell into anorexia, and in some cases starved themselves to death.

Authentic asceticism used practices that deepened self-awareness. The desert ascetic understood that growth in self-awareness was a necessary and valued component of the spiritual journey. Self-awareness was pursued through ascetical practices in order to become more deeply united with God and closer to heaven.

As the ammas taught, inner hesitancy and resistance to meeting God in honesty, silence, and solitude are related to our resistance to know ourselves in our frailties. An honest encounter with God challenges our capacity for intimacy. We may come to discover that we fear our passion for God. We may want to run from our sense of emptiness. Self-awareness calls us to face our hurt and anger. Above all else, self-awareness reveals our idols—those self-serving, false images of God that deny who God actually is.

THE DESERT WAY

Biblical scholar Walter Brueggemann speaks of the capacity of the Psalms to move us from orientation, through disorientation, and return us to a new reorientation.[4] We experience times of equilibrium, but when God moves us into a space of dislocation and relocation, beautiful psalms are birthed. In many ways this same experience is embodied in the life of the desert seeker. The ascetic was thrust into disorientation by accepting and embracing the gospel call to be lived out in the desert or monastery. Following each new experience of reorientation, the desert ascetic would be thrust again into disorientation through continued ascetical practices, moving ever closer to deep unity with God. This movement stripped the seeker of all that separated the truest self from God. This process of purification cultivated humility, compassion, purity of heart, and *apatheia*.

Apatheia

The goal of the desert journey was *apatheia*, the quality of the interior spiritual journey in which the inner struggle against inordinate attachments has ceased. Grounded in profound interior freedom, the ascetic was free of the strong pulls of worldly desires. Apatheia[5] is a mature mindfulness, a grounded sensitivity, and a keen attention to one's inner world as well as to the world in which one has journeyed. Strong emotions such as anger, fear, or anxiety did not dominate or control the ascetic's inner world; they were disciplined to serve the inner journey rather than disrupt it.

Apatheia is purity of heart. The ammas teach us to intentionally let go of all that keeps us from the single-minded pursuit of God: feelings and thoughts that bind us, cravings and addictions that diminish our sense of worth, and attachments to self-imposed perfectionism. Apatheia is nourished by simplicity grounded in abundance of the soul. This simplicity is in balance and harmony with the human community and the created world. To cultivate apatheia, we must be uncluttered in mind and heart and continue to be watchful and vigilant about those "seeping boundaries" where we can be deceived out of simplicity and into complexity under the guise of a "good."

Solitude, Hospitality, and Relationships

Although solitude was deeply valued and actively cultivated, the desert ascetic received all guests with a deep spirit
of hospitality. With the guest, Christ was received. Hence,
one's fast might be set aside to join a guest in a light meal.
Silence would be broken for heart-to-heart conversation. The
guest might later be taught to sit silently in the presence of
God while enjoying one another's company.

Desert ascetics understood that the journey to a deep
and mature relationship with God is made within oneself.
It is the arduous work of stripping away illusions and all that
keeps the ascetic from knowing that God gifted her with a
deep sense of understanding her own true humanity. This
understanding of their true humanity, created fully in the
image and likeness of God and yet still on the journey toward
full maturity, made desert ascetics deeply humble people.

Humility, Suffering, and Compassion

As the ammas taught, the virtue of humility does not
diminish a person's sense of self-worth or dignity. Humility is
the maturing state of deepening in understanding the implications of the incarnation—God's presence in the world. The
humility of a deeply listening and docile heart enables one to
learn even from an apparently disastrous experience.

Desert ascetics faced suffering with both determination
and courage. They understood that suffering, which in Greek
they named *penthos*, was grounded in their attachments to
attitudes, thoughts, motives, relationships, and reputation.
Suffering was the avenue to freedom and detachment, maturity and humility. Suffering remained until they "let go." A
deep capacity for compassion often resulted.

Compassion brought the ascetics to deep understanding of the struggles of others, enabled them to see themselves in the lives of others, and removed any sense of distance or distinction. Desert ascetics vigorously rejected any judgmental or critical attitude. They teach us that awareness of our own weaknesses gives us an opportunity to deepen our compassion for the weaknesses of others. As we cultivate a tender, vulnerable, expansive heart that embraces the humanity of all, we see with new eyes—the eyes and heart of Christ.

PRAYER

A certain monastic went to the cell of Abba Arsenius in Scetis and looked through the window, and beheld the old one as if completely on fire....Late on Saturday evening the old one turned his back on the setting sun, and stretched out his arms towards heaven in prayer; and so Arsenius remained until the rising sun shone on his face. And then he sat down.[6]

Prayer was a continuous way of life in the desert. It was intentionally cultivated until it became second nature. Prayer involved the hard work of learning a new language—the language of heaven. For the ascetic, prayer was not merely the speaking of words. It was the heart yearning for God, reaching out in hopeful openness to being touched by God. Prayer was the Holy Spirit breathing through the inner spirit of the ascetic and returning to God with yearnings for intimacy.

The ascetic sought to cultivate a silent, passionate, and burning love for God experienced in deep and nurturing solitude. The atmosphere for rich prayer was a simple quiet voice, not a noisy inner crowd. Physical as well as inner stillness and quiet were necessary. The words of prayer were brief and straight from the heart. Praying the psalms, intercession, contemplation, and silent awareness of God's presence were all expressions of prayer in the desert and monastery.

The Word

The psalms were recited throughout the day, and ascetics strove to pray into the night as well. Reading the sacred word, as is understood from our Jewish heritage, was a bodily experience.[7] Ascetics did not simply chant the psalms. In their pondering of the word, they allowed it to permeate their inner being in order to pray from their gut. Desert ascetics were grounded in Sacred Scripture. Knowing there were multiple senses of any text, they rejected a rigid approach to understanding scripture.

Seeking to interiorize the word and make it a part of their very being, ascetics often began their desert journey in deep inner struggle to reflect upon, understand, and become one with the word. Reverenced as a source of life, the word was seen as having a capacity to awaken deep sensitivity and to transmit life energy. Meaning was found when word and life corresponded. Wrestling with God's word cultivated in the ascetic a way of understanding and reflecting on the world. The word shaped how they saw and interpreted their culture. The word was their source for discerning God's call of the church.

Accidie

Amma Theodora warned her followers that as they began their discipline of prayer, they would be attacked by *accidie*, the sense of boredom or dejection that comes without cause as a temptation in prayer. Accidie deters one from the inner journey and discourages one's inner struggle toward freedom. Theodora invited her followers to be tenacious in prayer and to trust the original desire for God. The boredom then would pass.

SILENCE

Drawn deeper into the desert, they are drawn deeper into solitude, deeper into themselves and at the same time deeper into community and deeper into God the ground of being, and thus closer to the ground of being within us, for the depth of being of each of us is as strange and alien, yet hauntingly as familiar, as the desert solitude.[8]

The desert ascetic pursued and cultivated silence. This was a silence pregnant with the presence of the Divine, the womb where the word grew. The goal of silence was the inner quiet of strength, not the total absence of words.

Silence was deemed as intrinsic to the desert journey as prayer. This silence was inner calm and serenity grounded in strength. As for us today, silence calms the inner spirit to allow the whisperings of God to be heard. Silence allows the word to permeate to the inner heart. Purifying and nurturing silence supports the intentional inner journey.

Silence helps us begin the pilgrimage within and better discern the sacred. Silence helps us cultivate and deepen our passionate love for God because it provides the atmosphere of true and authentic communication with God. Silence teaches us to speak simply, directly, compassionately, and honestly. Kenneth Leech reminds us that "the protest of the solitary is not against human companionship as such, but against the evasion of self which can easily occur when involvement with people obscures and prevents any real encounter with one's own identity. Only in stillness can the truth be seen."[9]

Entering into silence is not easy. To risk encountering our fullest and truest self, and to meet God *as God is* requires courage and the freedom to risk. Silence invites us to meet and discover our truest selves—with masks, illusions, and public personae removed. Self-image is stripped and realigned: we begin to put on the mind of Christ. Silence, therefore, invites us to change, to grow toward the fullness of life. Silence helps us cultivate a healthy detachment from reputation, thwarted desires and plans, and anything that keeps us distracted from God.

The ascetic strove to sit quietly, attune her attention fully to the silence, and allow silence to speak its wisdom. As the Psalmist tells us, "But I have stilled and quieted my soul, like a weaned child with its mother, like a weaned child is my soul within me" (Ps 131:2).

For the desert dweller, "silence itself was layered, having depth and texture, and that to learn to be attentive to the varied qualities of the layers was to begin to discern the presence of the Spirit of God."[10] Silence is essentially listening.

LISTENING

Spiritual listening is a contemplative undertaking and not a problem solving task. It is essentially prayer....Spiritual listening as a contemplative discipline pushes us...to a level of listening beyond our own powers of analysis to the grace and the gift of divine life itself....To listen this way is to listen with heart and mind opened wide. It invites us to be changed along with those to whom we listen.[11]

Desert ascetics cultivated a heart engaged in intense listening. Listening for the Beloved's voice cultivated a wise and compassionate heart, able to yield to the movements of the Holy Spirit. Listening for the ebbs and flows of the Spirit was fundamental to a life of discernment. A still, focused attention was needed for fruitful discernment. True discernment does not presuppose how the Spirit will move, nor what God will say. In this life of cultivated listening, ascetics were open to the unexpected. They were willing to risk being surprised.

Desert ascetics were deeply aware that their cultural backgrounds, educations, and life experiences framed and influenced listening. Some were concerned that their prior education and privilege would hamper their inner journeys. Ammas steeped their minds in scripture and other sacred writings in order to cultivate minds and hearts able to listen for God's voice. Growth in self-awareness clarified the lens that filtered and colored their listening. The clearness of a prism was the goal.

Wendy Wright reminds us that listening in the desert tradition "involves listening to the delicate intersection of the human heart, with its desires and dreams, and the vast and silent mystery that is God."[12]

Chapter Three

THE SAYINGS OF THE DESERT MOTHERS

INTRODUCTION

Pilgrimage has been an important form of worship from the earliest days of Christianity. Traveling to the holy sites and visiting with the spiritual giants of the day have been highly valued experiences. The journals and letters of pilgrims record much of our early history. When approaching a spiritual master, the pilgrim would ask for a *word*—a word spoken by a desert ascetic under the inspiration of God. The word was given because the seeker was willing to put it into action.

Pilgrims, their souls stirred, began to share their received words with one another and with their faith communities at home. Disciples of spiritual masters also remembered words received and would later share them with their own followers. These words soon formed a rich oral tradition.

The sayings grew in number and were shared along trade routes.[1] Most often a group of sayings was attributed to a particular master. Unlike today, the Mediterranean culture of the time was an oral culture. While we can trust that these words are true, we know that the disciples and pilgrims were more concerned with remembering and sharing the essence and teaching received rather than with an exact word-for-word recitation.

In the fifth century, these sayings, originally spoken in the Coptic of Egypt, began to be written down, primarily in the Gaza region of Palestine where many of the Egyptian monks driven from home resettled. Desert ascetics and monastic communities had scattered because of ongoing theological debates.[2] Different versions of the same sayings appeared in different languages, some containing more sayings than others. The sayings are generally short, pithy, and cryptic, close in form to parables and folk wisdom, and are meant to stir the heart and give the hearer something to mull over.

Common themes of the sayings[3] are the importance of repentance and compunction, penance and obedience, which the ascetics called *penthos*; prayer and stillness, perseverance in the lifelong struggle to see God and become a friend to God, particularly a love for the cell, which they called *topos*; growth in self-awareness, silence and meditation, which they called *prosoche*; passionate desire for God and humble acceptance of God's love for us that leads to compassion for others, which they called *eros*; savoring the word of God and attentive listening to that word, which they called *logos*; and embodying the faint presence of paradise in our midst, of trying to become like the angels, which they called *telos*. Alongside the belief that their desert journey must be grounded in humility was their sense of self-emptying especially in the face of overwhelming suffering while acknowledging an all-loving God, in imitation of Christ, which the ascetics called *kenosis*.[4]

A restless heart was contrasted with an inner well of peace, strength, and stability. With their sayings, the desert ascetics sought to strip seekers of illusions and self-deceptions, enabling them to reject all that bound and constrained, and deepen their experience of true freedom. Genuine asceticism was grounded in the seeking heart.

Our Western and postmodern minds may find these sayings harsh. Desert ascetics knew from experience that they needed to shake the seeker awake as if from a stupor. They also understood that the inner journey was hard and required focused intent and discipline, like an athlete training for the Olympics.

In their sayings the desert ascetics often refer to "demons." Demons, or unclean spirits, were real and personal experiences for the early Christians. As the seeker entered the solitude of the desert or a small monastic community, the quiet allowed their minds to wander freely, generating a considerable flow of images, thoughts, and shifting emotions.[5] The ascetics found themselves confronted with a wide range of strong emotions, past memories, and unresolved issues that were all attributed to demonic possession. The desert monastic tradition was that these demons were essential to their inner transformation. They did not try to escape them; rather, they faced these strong urges head on. This process of self-emptying the ascetics called *kenosis*. The strength found in humility for desert ascetics was key.

Discernment of spirits was central to monastic teachings. Was this of God? From God? From the Evil One? How am I called to respond? Desert ascetics listened for the guidance of the Holy Spirit. Listening and humility were key to their ability to discern the presence of "demons."

In some ways we are no different today. Anyone who takes the call to transformation seriously, who cultivates some degree of silence in their life, will come crashing into their own "demons." In the wrestling and in seeking a wise elder, we become more compassionate and gain wisdom. The capacity to focus our minds and to block out unwanted and unhelpful mental distractions allows us to open an inner space for the Divine. This focused attention allows our spirits to move freely toward God—contemplative prayer. Today we nuance our understanding of human biology, normal sexual drives, and psychology with the inner call to make responsible and committed decisions. We still wrestle with our demons. We understand that to be tempted is common and normal.

These sayings were meant to be evocative, not merely descriptive or prescriptive, in order to elicit a deeper response from the listener. The amma gave words that would be wrestled with, cultivated, and reflected on in prayer, words that deeply impressed the mind and heart, words that spoke to the imagination and touched feelings. She sought to expose all barriers to a deeper experience of God. These sayings inspire us to stay single-minded in our pursuit of God and to deepen our capacity for love.

THE SAYINGS OF THE DESERT MOTHERS

Amma Matrona

This amma's Sayings have traditionally been included in various texts of the desert ascetics, but scholars have little knowledge and less certainty about her personal history. She most likely resided in the Egyptian desert.

The Sayings of Amma Matrona

1. We carry ourselves wherever we go, and we cannot escape temptation by mere flight.

Too many of us know the pain of fleeing relationships or work situations, thinking we can change what we hate within ourselves by relocating or fleeing our commitments. We are who we are wherever we go. Want to escape temptation? Or those parts of ourselves that we don't like? Then the work begins within us, to change attitudes, motives, and values. Desert ascetics advise us to seek a wise person to discern the choices that will close the doors on temptation, or to become the person we want to be. We do not have to live trapped in any hell, including one of our own making.

2. Many people living secluded lives on the mountain have perished by living like people in the world. It is better to live in a crowd and want to live a solitary life than to live a solitary life but all the time be longing for company.

How often have we found ourselves with chatter in our heads when we try to settle down and focus, whether on work or in prayer? The myriad ways we deluded ourselves that "somewhere else" was better than where we are now? The journey is inward away from noise and haste to a better awareness of who we are before God. Inner silence and calm is the goal, no matter where we are—in the city or in solitude.

Amma Sarah

Amma Sarah was a native of Upper Egypt. Born into a wealthy Christian family, Sarah was well educated and a voracious reader. Moving to the vicinity of a women's monastery in the desert of Pelusium (near Antinoë), Sarah lived alone for many years near the river in a cell with a terraced roof. She attended to the needs of the nearby community. Scholars believe she may have been a contemporary of Paphnutius of Thebes (d. 360 CE).

Eventually, Amma Sarah received the monastic garb and lived in a closer relationship with the community, serving as spiritual elder. She continued to follow the ascetic life by living alone in a cave by the river for seven years and died around her eightieth year.

Amma Sarah was deeply concerned that her heart never be divided in her pursuit of God. Much of her desert struggle was centered on calming inner distractions and cultivating those things that brought her close to God. "Lust" and "fornication" were not so much about bodily passions but rather anything or anyone that kept her heart distracted from God. The movement toward a deeper and more profound awareness of God spirals toward the simplicity that occurs when we voluntarily let go of all our attachments that keep us from moving deeper within. This is not a rejection of the created world, all of which is God's delightful gift to us, but rather is the rejection of our tendencies to grasp aspects of creation in a way that diminishes our unity with God.

Amma Sarah's goal was purity of heart, which is a singular focus on the inner journey. As one grows and deepens in purity of heart, one deepens in pure love for Christ. Sarah lived with a deep sense of awe for God. She sought neither special treatment nor recognition for herself.

Amma Sarah modeled for us the gift of tenacity and focus on the final goal of life: oneness with God. Sarah sought to eliminate distractions that she experienced as stumbling blocks to total union. This is never an easy journey, and Sarah's response was to pray for strength to endure and move into freedom. She avoided neither the challenges nor the pain. She stayed with her struggles until there was resolution.

Amma Sarah called her followers to growth in self-awareness. Self-awareness is not selfishness but self-connectedness. It is a deep and intense listening to our inner being, learning to be conscious and alert to what our inner world is trying to say to us. With self-awareness and self-knowledge, we understand our reactions toward others, issues that complicate our lives, blind spots that we can fall into, as well as our particular strengths and gifts. As we grow in self-awareness, we grow in God-awareness. Amma Sarah, in the desert tradition, understood that God has chosen humanity along with all creation as the vehicle of divine revelation.

Her feast day is July 13.

The Sayings of Amma Sarah

1. It was related of Amma Sarah that for thirteen years she waged warfare against the demon of sexual sin. She never prayed that the warfare should cease, but she said, "O God, give me strength."

Although Sarah may have been a deeply passionate woman, keenly aware of her sexuality, *sexual sin* principally meant anything that possessed her heart and separated her from God. Are we aware of what possesses our heart? A part of our being belongs only to God and can only be satisfied by God. Replacing God with anyone or anything is idolatry. Sarah, in her awareness of her own weaknesses and of God as the source of her strength, challenges us not to run but to stand firm in our persistent struggle with personal problems and with all that keeps us from God.

2. Once the same spirit of sexual sin attacked her more insistently, reminding her of the vanities of the world. But she gave herself up to the fear of God and to asceticism and went up onto her little terrace to pray. Then the spirit of sexual sin appeared bodily to her and said, "Sarah, you have overcome me." But she said, "It is not I who have overcome you, but my master, Christ."

Amma Sarah knew that we are always open to temptation, no matter how long we have been intent on our inner journey. She knew the source of her strength in a very earthy and incarnational way. She did not overcome this spirit of sexual sin on her own strength but trusted God to complete her journey into wholeness. Amma Sarah encourages us to cooperate with God's work and not rely solely on our own efforts.

3. It was said concerning her that for sixty years she lived beside a river and never lifted her eyes to look at it.

Amma Sarah lived along the Nile River. Not easily distracted, she allowed her surroundings to support her without any need to possess them. She so intensely focused on cultivating total union with God that it seems she was unaware of her surroundings. What distracts us? Can we pull our gaze away from electronic devices and social media to free up time for contemplative prayer?

4. Another time, two elders, great ones, came to the district of Pelusia to visit her. When they arrived, one said to the other, "Let us humiliate this old woman." So they said to her, "Be careful not to become conceited thinking to yourself: 'Look how anchorites are coming to see me, a mere woman.'" But Amma Sarah said to them, "According to nature I am a woman, but not according to my thoughts."

To be a woman was to be "fleshly, sinful, sensuous, passionate, and bodily": qualities Sarah's culture sought to avoid. To be a man was to be "rational, godlike, angelic, otherworldly": qualities valued in her culture. To be "manly" (not necessarily a male) was to live beyond the passions: to know them, to be aware of them, yet not let them rule. Several of our spiritual foremothers were referred to by their contemporaries as "this female man of God"—and this was deemed a compliment! Amma Sarah was aware of the depth of her spirituality. She did not need the approval of anyone for who she was or for the inner journey she had undertaken. Not willing to be diminished by foolish and arrogant men, she gifted them with an appropriate reply.

This is an invitation to let go of concern for our reputation. What others think of us is none of our business. While it might be difficult to detach from others' opinions of us, in letting go we will know profound freedom to be ourselves and to better hear the leading of the Holy Spirit in our lives.

5. Amma Sarah said, "If I prayed to God, asking that all people find fulfillment *in me*, I will be found at the door of each one of them, asking for forgiveness. No, I will instead pray to have a pure heart with everyone."

Amma Sarah did not allow herself to be burdened by others' expectations of her. She reminded her followers that if she did, she would fall short and therefore need to apologize. Likewise, she remained nonjudgmental in her attitude toward others and their own journey toward God. She sought to remain true to her own simple path toward God. So can we.

6. She also said, "I put out my foot to ascend the ladder, and I place death before my eyes before going up it."

Ascending and descending a ladder was a well-known metaphor in Amma Sarah's day.[6] To ascend a ladder was to draw close to God and deepen in spiritual maturity. The metaphors of the ladder and of keeping death ever before one's eyes figure strongly in desert and monastic spirituality. We are exhorted to remain firmly focused on our search for God. Being mindful of death makes it imperative to live each day to the fullest. There may not be a tomorrow. What might it mean for us if we live as if today is all we have? What would be our priorities? This can free us to make mindful choices that support and nurture the goal: abiding in God's unconditional love.

7. She also said, "It is good to give to people in need, even if it's so people can see what you're doing, because even if you do it to please people, it will come to please God, too."

Early ascetics deeply valued having something to give to the poor and were consistent in their giving. Manual labor was both a part of their ascetic practice as well as a means of providing for the poor, but the value was love.

Amma Sarah acknowledged that our initial attempts at giving alms may be driven by mixed motives but eventually we are converted by the poor and by our almsgiving. Any place is a place to begin.

Mindfulness of the poor, the marginalized, and the oppressed cultivates within us a deeper capacity to experience God's endless compassion for us and for all creation. It is in extending compassion to others that we both experience and receive God's compassion. These incarnational experiences begin to teach us of God.

8. Some monks of Scetis came one day to visit Amma Sarah. She offered them a small basket of fruit. They left the good fruit and ate the bad. So she said to them, "You are the true monks of Scetis."

Desert asceticism does not seek to draw attention to self. Ascetical practices were quiet and unobtrusive. The desert ascetic practiced self-denial in small daily ways, such as choosing simpler and less appetizing foods, just enough sleep on a sufficient but not necessarily comfortable bed, and prayers spread throughout the day. Self-denial was cultivated to deepen one's relationship to God, to deepen in compassion, and to build bridges to others.

The true ascetic seeks neither to exalt nor to denigrate

self. Humility is to know oneself as created by God, as interdependent with others and the cosmos, and deeply loved by God. Humility helps us to embrace and deepen our sense of connectedness. Are we content having less? Of seeking to live simply? To not draw attention to ourselves?

> 9. She also said to the brothers, "It is I who am a man, you who are women."

The "brothers" intended an insult as women were considered naturally inferior to men. Following the gospel mandate to "turn the other cheek" she twisted their words in a paradox and claimed her integrity. Amma Sarah knew who she was and did not waver—this is genuine humility. She both challenges the arrogance of presuming one is better than another due to gender, education, position in society, or anything else, and challenges her hearers to pursue spiritual maturity.

Are we aware of ways we might consider someone else "lesser" and assume a position of superiority? Of elitism? Will we allow the Holy Spirit to expose our bigotries and blindness?

Amma Syncletica of Egypt

> For just as those who wish to gaze at the sun damage their vision, so also those who try to mirror the radiance of her life fall victim to confusion of mind, dazzled, overcome, and unstrung by the magnitude of her achievements.[7]

We know of Amma Syncletica from the Sayings as well as from *The Life and Regimen of the Blessed and Holy Teacher Syncletica*, a fifth-century work by Pseudo-Athanasius.[8] The early church thought her so important that her Life survives to this day. Evagrius Ponticus, an early theologian of mysticism, influenced her teachings.[9]

Amma Syncletica was born in Alexandria into a respected Christian family of Macedonian heritage. Her two brothers died at relatively young ages and her sister was blind. She was well educated and had a reputation for her beauty. Syncletica began her ascetical practices in her parents' home.

When her parents died, Amma Syncletica sold all her possessions and distributed the family wealth among the poor. She then cut her hair as a sign of consecration and moved with her blind sister to the family tomb outside Alexandria. Here she began her life as a desert ascetic.

As women began to gather around her, Amma Syncletica reluctantly agreed to serve as their spiritual mentor, training them in the disciplines of the inner life. She trained her followers to cultivate such qualities as gentleness, patience, and endurance—qualities grounded in love and vitally needed for a fruitful spiritual journey.

For Syncletica, this discipline meant emptying oneself of all stumbling blocks: attitudes, motives, addictions, emotions not united with Christ, as well as any ignorance that hindered the inner journey. Amma Syncletica sought to relinquish anger, vindictiveness, envy, and ambition, and challenged her followers to do the same. Through her Life and Sayings, she encourages us to grow in self-awareness, to understand our passions and desires, and to purify them, always directing us toward God.

Amma Syncletica lived into her eighties and died after three and a half years of intense physical suffering, most likely from cancer.

Her feast day is January 5.

The Sayings of Amma Syncletica

1. Amma Syncletica said, "It is a struggle and very hard work for those who are drawing closer to God—at first. But then comes indescribable joy. Those who want to light a fire first get assailed by

smoke and weep and, by doing this, obtain the desired fire; in the same way we too have to kindle the divine fire for ourselves with tears and afflictions since it says 'Our God is a consuming fire.'"[10]

Amma Syncletica was aware that change is often painful. She was honest with her followers yet gave them hope that the hard work of conversion—of the spiritual battle—brings joy with it as well. In desert spirituality, change can mean becoming countercultural, altering family dynamics and lifestyles, which can result in suffering of one kind or another. This suffering was deeply personal, especially when necessary choices affected those who did not understand the desert journey.

Amma Syncletica understood these difficulties. Initial attempts at asceticism can be rough and seem to bear little fruit. Old support systems begin to disappear, and the new journey seems clumsy and foreign. The spiritual journey seems filled with digression rather than progression forward. Discouragement can easily settle in. Amma Syncletica exhorts us not to give up hope.

2. She also said, "We who have taken on and profess this way of life must hold fast in the strongest way possible to good judgment, moderation, and self-control. To be sure, these virtues seem to be exercised by those in the world but, right alongside them, with those in the world come bad judgment, immoderate behavior, and lack of self-control because they sin with all their other senses. It is a fact: they look at things in an unsuitable way and laugh in an irresponsible manner."

Our speech and eyes are the mirrors of our soul. Amma Syncletica was concerned that too much boisterous behavior reveals an unbalanced inner world. Balanced moderation is thoughtful and nurturing and integrates the essentials of our lives. Desert ascetics teach that balance in all aspects of our lives is a necessary condition for a fruitful inner journey. Acknowledging that some degree of balance can be found in anyone's life, Amma Syncletica challenges her followers to be single-minded about building and maintaining a nurturing balance. It is in the inner space created by our temperance that fruitful growth and transformation occur. Paradoxically, maintaining balance is harder for many than undisciplined behavior.

3. She also said, "Just as the most bitter medicine drives out poisonous creatures, so prayer joined to fasting drives evil thoughts away."

Although the desert way was of sparse meals and fasting from most foods, Amma Syncletica understood that more was involved. Fasting may take the form of giving up something other than food, such as excessive commitments, overachiev-ing, unhealthy attitudes, and old resentments. The desert ascetics began by fasting from food, possessions, and social relationships.[11] They then progressed to fasting from interior attachments, such as anger, jealousy, envy, or possessiveness. The desert ascetics understood that fasting creates the space in our bodies, minds, and spirits for God to *be* within us, for new things to grow.

The ammas knew the power of thoughts: to encourage, affirm, be creative, move, and nourish. They can also move one toward discouragement, despair, anxiety, and depression. Fasting and prayer breaks the cycle of thoughts that drains one of life; prayer heals and nourishes the inner life. Faith enables one to trust that an inner work is going on even when there are no corresponding positive feelings or when difficulties are encountered.

4. She also said, "Do not let yourself be seduced by the delights of the riches of the world, as though they contained something useful on account of vain pleasure. Worldly people esteem the culinary art, but you, through fasting and thanks to cheap food, go beyond their abundance of food. It is written: 'One who is sated loathes honey' [Prov 27:7]. Do not fill yourself with bread and you will not desire wine."

Overindulgence drags and weighs us down, dulls self-awareness, weakens our inner strength and resolve, and can cause us to lose sight of the pursuit of our original goal. Overindulgence can be a sign that we seek to replace God with something else.

Amma Syncletica beckons us into true freedom, freedom that does not rely on external things for inner happiness and peace. The early ascetics valued simplicity, modesty, and acceptance of their physical situations. They sought balance in their daily lives, aware that they were on a long journey.

5. Blessed Syncletica was asked if it is a perfect good to go without possessions. She said, "For those who are capable of it, it is a perfect good. Those who can endure this do bear with physical affliction but receive suffering in the body but rest in the soul, for just as one washes coarse clothes by trampling them underfoot and turning them about in all directions, even so the strong soul becomes much more stable thanks to voluntary poverty."

Simplicity keeps us faithful to the spiritual journey and removes anything that keeps us from God. Simplicity supports and strengthens our deepest commitments and responsibilities.

Balance helps us recognize when poverty is becoming an idol in itself. The ascetic does not seek poverty for poverty's sake but rather cultivates simplicity for the sake of the poor and to remove any blockages to finding God.

As we move through life, we often sense a call toward simplicity: not just of our possessions but of our commitments, attitudes, and whatever binds our heart. As we become more aware of what possesses us, we yearn to divest ourselves of this. Stress is often a good indicator of our need to simplify.

6. She also said, "If you find yourself in a monastery do not go to another place, for that will harm you a great deal. Just as the bird who abandons the eggs she was sitting on prevents them from hatching, so the monk or the nun grows cold and their faith dies, when they go from one place to another."

Did you make a significant change in your life—a relationship, a job, a change of residence—because you were discontented? Bored? Yearning for something, but did not take time to discern what you hungered for? Amma Syncletica challenges her followers to stay put. The desert journey is one inch long and many miles deep. Inward is the only direction of travel.

The spiritual journey requires perseverance, steadfastness, remaining with commitments, and working through difficulties. Relationships can grow stale and boring; our excessive commitments can seem hard to untangle. "Moving on" might seem easier than working through misunderstandings; "staying on" is an invitation to deepen valued relationships and commitments.[12] Stability and perseverance provide the strength for the hard interior work of transformation; inner wrestling deepens our interior life. Amid this hard work we encounter our real selves.

7. She also said, "The Devil has numerous ways to ambush us. If he has not shifted the soul through poverty? He offers wealth as bait. If he does not prevail through insults and rebukes? He ostentatiously makes a show of offering compliments and the idea of glory. Has he been defeated by good health? He afflicts the body with illness. If he has been unable to beguile a person offering pleasures, he tries to lead him stray by causing unwanted sufferings. It is a fact that he supplies certain grievous maladies as he wishes so that through them, he can shake up those who because of them are growing faint-hearted in their love for God.

"But even when your body is cut and slashed by raging fever and suffering with unquenchable thirst, if you as a sinner bear under these afflictions, keep in mind the retribution to come and the eternal fire and judicial punishments and by no means become fainthearted at the way things are now. Rejoice that God is exercising care and supervision over you and keep that renowned saying on your lips: 'The Lord has disciplined and instructed me, but he has not handed me over to death' [Ps 118:8].

"You have become iron, but through fire you are sloughing off iron's rust. And if you get sick even though you are righteous, you are advancing from great things to even greater ones. You are gold, but through fire you are becoming even more tried and true. A messenger was given to you with regard to the flesh. Rejoice? Look at whom you have come to resemble! You have become worthy to share in Paul's portion. Through fiery fever you have been tried and tested; through shivering with cold you have been disciplined. But scripture says 'We went through fire and water and you have brought us to where we feel relief and can rest' [Ps 66:12].

"Have you been through the former? Wait for the latter. As you practice virtue, cry out the words of the holy one: he says 'Poor and suffering am I' [Ps 69:29]. You will become full-grown and mature through these two afflictions; this is so because it says 'In affliction you have made me more open.' Rather than focusing on our troubles, let us train the soul with spiritual disciplines. Hers is the truth: we can see the Adversary right in front of our eyes."

Reread this passage slowly, listening for where you might have experienced similar sufferings. We have all experienced painful and difficult seasons in our life. Do we recognize the opportunity for growth? Come to a deeper understanding of ourselves and who God is for us as a result of these trials?

Desert spirituality understood that the spiritual journey was one of spiritual warfare. Ascetics called this *kenosis*: a wrenching suffering and emptying and pointed their students to the Paschal Mystery.[13] Any weapon might be used against the seeker. Amma Syncletica was known for her profound gifts of the discernment of spirits. She had a keen perception of what was going on in someone's inner struggles.

Any situation can be used by the evil one to distract and confuse us, discourage us, and try to move us toward despair or apathy. Any situation can be an opportunity for learning and growth. For Amma Syncletica, a "sinner" is one who allows circumstances to disrupt prayerful pursuit of God or who gives up the inner journey altogether. Detachment allows us the reflective space and inner freedom to recognize these attacks and learn from them. Keeping the eye of our soul upon our ultimate goal helps us not to get hooked by the turbulence of daily life.

The evil one attacks our sense of self-worth and feeds our internalized self-hatred.[14] Discouragement and depression can move us toward despair and a loss of hope in God. When we live out of our wounded sense of self-worth, we tend not to trust the inner wisdom and intuition given each of us by God.

8. She also said, "If illness weighs us down, let us not be distressed as though, because of the illness and the prostration of our bodies, we could not sing as we normally do, for all these things are for our good, for the purification of our desires. Truly fasting and sleeping on the ground are set before us because of our sensuality. If illness then weakens this sensuality, the reason for these practices is superfluous. For this is the great asceticism: to remain steadfast in illness and to sing hymns of thanksgiving to God."

Illness is not pleasant. Many of us have experienced debilitating illness either of a temporary or chronic nature. How we respond to illness says much about the state of our relationship with God. Might we trust God? Deepen our prayerful reliance on God's providential care?

Amma Syncletica was concerned that her followers grow and deepen in their understanding of the inner journey. Bodily asceticism serves to focus our single-minded pursuit of God by deepening our self-awareness and God-awareness. Tempering our body deepens our capacity to live in freedom, a freedom that allows us to experience and express our passion for God sensuously, without confusing our sensuality with the totality of our being.

Although Amma Syncletica was primarily concerned with singing the psalms and praising God, she also invites us to find new ways to explore our understanding of our singing. Illness, disabilities, or circumstances may hinder or thwart us, but this should not silence us. Singing expresses our innermost yearnings and desire for God.

9. She also said, "While fasting, do not use illness as an excuse to stop: to be sure, those who do not fast often succumb to various kinds of sickness. Have you begun to do good? Do not flinch now when the Enemy blocks your path: even he is made powerless by patient endurance."

When those who set out sailing first encounter a favorable wind, they unfurl the sails; later, when they meet an opposing wind, the sailors do not abandon their sailing because they have happened upon it. They sit still for a while or even fight against the surging of the sea, and then once again continue sailing. It is the same with us: when an opposing wind comes against us, instead of unfurling sails, let us set up the cross and freely complete our journey.

The early years of our spiritual journey are often filled with wonderful experiences of God. Great strides are made in prayer and personal transformation, the very near presence of God seems to be with us daily, and the miraculous is seen. Then the journey seems to get harder. Growth and transformation come to frustrating dead ends. Prayer seems dry and pointless. Friends, at best, fail to understand us and too often abandon us—family can too. Sometimes it seems that God has abandoned us. Amma Syncletica wants us to remember that these "tempest times" will come, but they will also pass by.

Amma Syncletica urges us to remember the God who is our strength and support during these difficult times. Our spiritual disciplines are for our own benefit. Our spiritual practice strengthens our resolve to remain undeterred in our pursuit of spiritual transformation and fosters the inner shifts needed in our attitudes and motives. We are better able to seek God. Jesus is our assurance that we have not been abandoned. Jesus is our best example of how we can stand firm amid the turbulence.

10. She also said, "Those who have endured the labors and dangers of the sea and then amass material riches, even when they have gained much desire to gain yet more. They consider what they have at present as nothing and reach out for what they have not got. We, who have nothing that we desire, wish to acquire everything through the fear of God."

Are we satisfied with what we have? With what we have accomplished? If not, then discern what that dissatisfaction is about. Be honest with yourself. Dissatisfaction is often, at its core, a spiritual hunger. Desert spirituality understood that with each new dawn, there was the new beginning. Amma Syncletica exhorted her followers not to accept easily gained substitutes for authentic union with God.

The ascetic knows the riches sought, and in remembering this is not easily swayed. Anything else fails to satisfy and leaves us sated but wanting more. We will experience times of great inner emptiness. It can be tempting to fill this emptiness with anything and everything, but unless it is God, we will be unsatisfied. Nurturing and prayerful reflection upon our experiences of emptiness invites us to move deeper within and to mature spiritually.

11. She also said, "Imitate the tax collector so you will not be condemned with the Pharisee, and choose the gentleness and humility of Moses in order to transform your flinty heart into springs of running water."

Desert spirituality valued mercy, grounded in humble awareness of personal need. Desert spirituality also understood that meekness — grounded in the strength and courage of the desert — would be rewarded with life.

The qualities of gentleness, kindness, and humility foster awareness of our need for God and the openness to be taught by God. Paradoxically, each fosters self-acceptance: neither greater nor lesser than our neighbor. Amma Syncletica challenged her followers to embrace themselves in their createdness and creatureliness before God, dwelling in a stance of open vulnerability that can be taught and shown the way.

12. She also said, "It is dangerous for anyone to teach who has not been raised up through practice and experience. For example, if someone with a dilapidated house welcomes strangers, harm is done if the house collapses. It is the same with these teachers: if they do not first lay a foundation for themselves, they will ruin those who come to them to be taught. With the teacher's words, those who have come for teaching have been summoned for salvation but, instead, the teachers, through the evil way they behave, have wronged these combatants."

Desert ascetics did not seek students. They were keenly aware of the responsibility that they had for their disciple. A true ascetic tended to resist accepting a follower into her cell, and hence, her life. Amma Syncletica has strong words for those who would be called "teacher." She gives her listeners some guidelines for discerning a true spiritual elder. An elder was first taught by a desert master and was shaped by life in the desert. Healing and wisdom were the fruit.

Desert ascetics valued authenticity, seeking to let it permeate their very being. Any teaching must be grounded in the ascetic's lived experiences. Her example and the integrity of her life give evidence of her interiority. Amma Syncletica understood that with an elder, there must be a consistency between words and life, and a sense of inner strength and calm. An amma's word moved followers toward a deeper sense of one's own personal relationship with God, rather than interfere with this relationship.

For us today, there is also an invitation and a certain urgency to network with kindred spirits: with those who deeply value the hard work of the inner journey. The guidelines for choosing an elder are still valid today.

> 13. She also said, "It is good not to get angry, but if this should happen, St. Paul does not allow you a whole day for this passion, for he says: 'Let not the sun go down' [Eph 4:25]. Will you wait till all your time is ended? Why hate the one who has grieved you? It is not this person who has done the wrong, but the evil one. Hate sickness but not the sick person."

Desert spirituality perceived anger as a deterrent to the inner journey and a wall to unity with God. Anger often revealed a lack of detachment, and certainly violated silence. If a disciple got angry, then Amma Syncletica wanted her followers to be aware of the difference between the person and sin.

We must deal with the cause of our anger: acknowledge the gift and message of anger and respond to what our anger is calling forth in us. If we do not actively attend to our anger, it comes out in ugliness such as bitterness, resentment, rage, and depression. Unfortunately, we can just sit around and nurture our anger, stroke it into resentment, and get negative energy from passively attending to it.

If we are willing to actively listen to what our anger would tell us, we can then act on what we must do: seek reconciliation, speak the truth, and/or make necessary changes in our life. Working with a spiritual companion or present-day amma to discern how to respond to our anger may be very helpful. It is not always obvious what we must do with our response to our anger. Reflection with a wise amma can help. For a heart seeking only God, there is no room for resentment.

> 14. She also said, "Those who are great athletes must contend against stronger enemies."

Desert spirituality understood a "great athlete" as one who took on longer fasts, more difficult prayer vigils, and greater experiences of solitude, often moving deeper into the desert. These "enemies" or contenders were those discoveries deep within the self that limited God-experience and God-understanding.

I have journeyed with people in spiritual direction who seem on the surface to have no great inner conflicts. They are also unsatisfied with their relationship with God. When we begin to explore their healthy passions and desires, when we look together at their healthy abilities to take risk, I often notice a correlation between a reluctance to risk expressing their gifts and an unsatisfactory relationship with God.

I have sat with those who wrestle with honest inner anguish, wondering where God is in the midst of it. I have been deeply aware and awed by how gifted these people are. As they wrestle with their understanding of God and their "God questions," it seems I am watching them give birth to a new self that will deeply bless the human community.

At times, our talents and abilities, given us by God for the benefit and joy of God's creation, can make the inner journey toward quiet and unity with God more difficult. Amma Syncletica recognized that her more gifted followers may have also faced deeper anguish as they sought to become one with God. I hear encouragement not to shy away from our gifts but to recognize the value of our inner struggles as we seek to become the people God intended us to be.

15. She also said, "There is an asceticism which is determined by the enemy and his disciples practice it. So how are we to distinguish between the divine and royal asceticism and the demonic tyranny? Clearly through its quality of balance. Always use a single rule of fasting. Do not fast four or five days and break it the following day with any amount of food. In truth, lack of proportion always corrupts. While you are young and healthy, fast, for old age with its weakness will come. As long as you can, lay up treasure, so that when you cannot, you will be at peace."

Demonic tyranny? Amma Syncletica was aware that there were some who went to extremes in their asceticism, even to the point of destroying their health. She did not want her followers to do this. It is too easy to fall into the deception that "harder is better." She understood that obsessions and perfectionism drive many people whose asceticism is not grounded in personal freedom.

Amma Syncletica called for her followers to balance asceticism grounded in reflective discernment. She encouraged her followers to pursue spiritual maturity and healthy ways of being that build wisdom. She was concerned with proper motive behind the ascetical practice. True ascetical practices empower our prayer, deepen our sense of serene peace, and move us closer to God and others.

16. She also said, "As long as we are in the monastery, obedience is preferable to asceticism. The one teaches pride, the other humility."

Obedience is faithful attending to the whispering guidance of the Spirit within ourselves as we listen to scripture,
tradition, our faith community, and those people intimately
involved in our lives. Obedience is active and fruitful and
evokes an intelligent response. Obedience does not silence
the prophetic voice — to speak the truth passionately from
the heart takes courage and obedience to the stirrings of the
Spirit.[15]

Obedience to the spiritual journey is neither simple
nor easy. The faith community God has placed us in can
disappoint us, provoke us to anger, or leave us dissatisfied.
Painfully — and truthfully — our family, friends, and faith community will invite us to see ourselves as we really are. Too
often it can seem that life would be easier if we moved on
rather than staying "for the long haul."

> 17. She also said, "We must direct our souls with dis-
> cernment. As long as we are in the monastery, we
> must not seek our own will, nor follow our per-
> sonal opinion, but obey our elders in the faith."

Discernment, essential in the teaching of the desert
ascetics, is vital to the spiritual journey. Discernment requires
that we listen deeply and intently to our hearts, and to all the
ways that God chooses to whisper to us. Saint Benedict tells
his followers to listen "with the ear of [their] hearts."[16] When
we listen well, we intentionally choose to hear those we dis-
agree with, those whose lives are significantly different from
ours, and we allow ourselves to be stretched and challenged.
There is a quality of openness to learn and to change.

It is through discernment that we come to better know our
truest self as well as the false self we have so heavily invested
in. Amma Syncletica is concerned that we cease empowering
our false self and instead risk the journey deep within to find
our truest self and God.

18. She also said, "It is written, 'Be wise as serpents and innocent as doves' [Matt 10:16]. Being like serpents means not ignoring attacks and wiles of the devil. Like is quickly known to like. The simplicity of the dove denotes purity of action."

Serpents are wise: they are aware of their hostile environment and are prepared to defend themselves from attack. In pursuit of purity of heart and singleness of intention, Amma Syncletica calls us to be attentive and aware of those things that can creep back into our lives and thwart our journey. When our attentiveness dulls, we are susceptible to attack and may begin the deceptive slide toward mediocrity. Amma Syncletica exhorts us to wise simplicity: to choose an uncomplicated life, to seek oneness with God, and yet to be mindful of how easy it is to be caught unawares.

19. Amma Syncletica said, "There are many who live in the mountains and behave as if they were in the town, and they are wasting their time. It is possible to be a solitary in one's mind while living in a crowd, and it is possible for one who is a solitary to live in the crowd of personal thoughts."

Alone with ourselves, we can still be crowded with rapid-fire thoughts, conflicting emotions, and concerns. We can be bombarded by the inner noise of internalized messages that are not from God and become exhausted by the internal churning that results from stress. Sometimes we seek out the company of others just to avoid this menacing internal crowd.

The journey to the desert begins in our heart. Movement toward simplicity begins within. Solitude is about inner silence, calm, being grounded—in our bodies, in our healthy relationships, and in our God. The desert is the place that supports our learning this. The desert reveals the inner turbulence that keeps us churned up and distracted.

> 20. She also said, "In the world, if we commit an offence, even an involuntary one, we are thrown into prison. Let us likewise cast ourselves into prison because of our sins, so that voluntary remembrance may anticipate the punishment that is to come."

Amma Syncletica invited her followers to journey into a voluntary prison: the place of inner reflection where we make an honest assessment of self and come to recognize those areas in our lives that need reform, reconciliation, and healing. She would have us cultivate awareness of our createdness, of our healthy dependence upon God, and of our interconnectedness with one another. This prison becomes the place of grace where transformation begins.

As we grow in self-awareness, we begin to become aware of the unnecessary prisons we have placed ourselves in. At times, these familiar prisons can seem more safe and secure than risking the journey out and into freedom. Jesus would lead us toward freedom, but he is gentle and calls us only when we are ready and willing to go.

> 21. She also said, "Just as a treasure that is exposed loses its value, so a virtue which is known vanishes. Just as wax melts when it is near fire, so the soul is destroyed by praise and loses all the results of its labor."

Desert spirituality is a hidden spirituality. Desert ascetics sought to "disappear" from the memory of others. To be seen by others was to fall from the chosen path. A virtue seen is a virtue lost.

Amma Syncletica was also aware that the inner journey is sensitive and tender. It is the place where we are most vulnerable to attack. It is the place where our true selves emerge, unknown and unproven. Because of an unconscious and innate need to protect that tender vulnerability, the inner journey is deeply susceptible to pride. Amma Syncletica alerted her disciples to this danger.

22. She also said, "Just as it is impossible to be at the same moment both a plant and a seed, so it is impossible for us to be surrounded by worldly honor and at the same time to bear heavenly fruit."

Most of us are a mosaic of maturity and immaturity. God creates us with wonderful potential: potential that needs tender nurturing and exposure to growth-filled experiences. When we patiently tend to our inner gardens, the seed of spirituality germinates. Growth, maturity, and fruitfulness are the result. Self-defeating, self-deceiving behaviors thwart this seed's attempts to grow, leaving us in stagnating immaturity.

Amma Syncletica consistently rejected worldly recognition. She was concerned that honors given by society may diminish ardent pursuit of the inner journey. Nothing was to detract us from the primacy of Jesus in our lives.

23. She also said, "My children, we all want to be saved, but because of our habit of negligence, we swerve away from salvation."

Amma Syncletica was not speaking of the "first" salvation found in embracing the message of Jesus of Nazareth; rather, she was concerned about a mature living out of salvation that is serious about following Jesus. Negligence is deceptive, often initially appearing to be "good." Seemingly innocuous choices can begin to snowball—we become unaware and inattentive in many ways. This is why we must be watchful and attentive, discerning the direction of our choices.

24. She also said, "We must arm ourselves in every way against the demons. For they attack us from outside, and they also stir us up from within; and the soul is then like a ship when great waves break over it, and at the same time it sinks because the hold is too full. We are just like that: we lose as much by the exterior faults we commit as by the thoughts inside us. So we must watch for the attacks from people that come from outside us, and also repel the interior onslaughts of our thoughts."

"Demons" were often mentioned in the language of the early church. Ascetics did not flee from demons but knew that wrestling with them made the ascetic stronger in faith. Discernment as to what was going on was essential to desert understanding of these inner struggles.

Early Christians did not have the language of psychology to describe their experiences of inner turmoil. Everything was attributed to demonic activity—true evil as well as personal sin or woundedness. In our attentiveness and watchfulness, Amma Syncletica invites us to be aware of the sources of our own inner turmoil: all those things that keep us distracted and out of focus, frustrated and drained of energy.

Amma Syncletica calls us to be aware of giving too much voice to our internalized self-hatred. When we become aware of those parts of our inner self that are vulnerable to attack from others, we can be prepared and less apt to be caught off guard. Internal and external attacks "feed" the messages we have internalized that tell us of our unworthiness, of our lack, of all that we are not and yet "should" be. This reinforces and perpetuates our internalized messages of self-hatred.

Amma Syncletica encourages us to be watchful and aware of how we respond when—not if—these attacks occur. In our self-awareness we can respond appropriately and care for ourselves in the midst of them.

> 25. She also said, "We are never free from cares here; it is as the scripture says: 'Let the person who thinks he is standing watch out that he does not fall' [1 Cor 10:12]. We sail in uncertain waters: The holy psalmist says that life is a sea, but some parts of the sea are rocky, some are infested by wild beasts, and some are calm.
>
> "We, then, seem to be sailing on the calm part of the sea while those living in the world are tossed about by waves; so, too we sail by day guarded by the sun of righteousness, while they, out of ignorance, sail by night. But—it is often possible that the person living in the world, sailing during winter and in darkness, can, by being vigilant, bring his own boat to safety. We, on the other hand, through negligence, although we are sailing in calm waters, by letting go of the rudder of righteousness can sink beneath the waves."

Attentiveness was a key value in desert spirituality. The art of attentiveness was actually much of the goal of monasticism, what the ascetics referred to as *prosoche*, an intense awareness or mindfulness of the present moment. It is with this cultivated gift of attentiveness that we can discern the leadings of the Holy Spirit and of "demons" or our shadow side that might lure us away from our spiritual journey.

Amma Syncletica was keenly aware that those who have been intentional about their inner journey and who have grown in their sense of inner calm and tranquility, can quickly grow lax and be caught off guard. We must never presume we have "arrived." The inner journey is a way of life, a process of transformation that continues until death.

There is also a deceptive calm when we do not attend to our inner world. True calm cannot be forced or willed into existence. Our lack of awareness of inner turmoil, or the call to growth, is not true calm. True inner calm is rooted in strength and reality. There is a sense of movement toward life, toward the Divine. Purity of motives and purity of heart are maintained.

> 26. She also said, "Just as a ship cannot be built without nails, so too is it impossible to be saved without humility."

Simply put, desert ascetics considered humility the foundation and cornerstone of the spiritual journey. Humility (not humiliation) is that basic stance that recognizes God is God and I am not, and that a humble person is one who recognizes that they have something to learn from others and even from life itself. The opposite of faith is not doubt;[17] rather, the opposite of faith is certitudes. People who live with their beloved certitudes tend to resist learning from others as that would mean admitting that they don't actually know it all. But mercy can and does intervene and the Holy Spirit finds a crack to slip in and disturb our well-constructed inner world.

> 27. She also said, "There is a beneficial sorrow and there is deadly sorrow: useful sorrow is to lament one's own sins and the illness of one's neighbor in order not to fail in one's resolve and plans but rather to lay one's hands on perfect goodness.
>
> "But there is also a sorrow that comes from the Enemy, completely irrational, which has

been called 'accedie' by some. Therefore, one needs to drive off this spirit with prayer and especially by singing psalms."

Healthy sorrow or grief is dynamic and transformative: it moves us deep within, and hopefully closer to God. Sorrow can help us to touch our well of compassion and extend it toward ourselves and others. Sorrow can also be an opportunity to allow ourselves to rest deeply in God's compassion.

Sorrow that feeds inner turmoil and refuses resolution, that moves us toward death rather than life, that leads us away from our truest selves, must be rooted out or healed. The Greek word *accedie*[18] translates as "I don't care," a kind of weariness or even disdain where the spiritual life is concerned. A person is giving up because the inner work seems too hard or difficult, or they're not seeing results. A spiritual director, mentor, or other professional can help us look at ways to let go of our grief issues and move on. We can discover resurrection in our grief.

Amma Theodora

Amma Theodora lived in the fourth century in the desert of Egypt. Not much is known about her, and at times, Amma Theodora has been confused with other women of the same name. We do know that she was a colleague of Archbishop Theophilus of Alexandria (d. 412 CE) and was often consulted by monastics about the monastic life.

Amma Theodora was concerned that her disciples have a self-discipline that would withstand inner and outer conflict. She also was one of the first persons to give a description of *accidie*.

Her feast day is September 1.

The Sayings of Amma Theodora

1. Amma Theodora asked Archbishop Theophilus about some words of the apostle, saying, "What does this mean, 'Knowing how to profit by circumstances'?" (Col 4:5). He said to her, "This saying shows us how to profit at all times. For example, is it a time of excess for you? By humility and patience buy up the time of excess and draw profit from it. Is it the time of shame? Buy it up by means of resignation and win it. So everything that goes against us can if we wish, become profitable to us."

Life is a continuous occasion for learning. Our interaction with and listening to others are opportunities to grow. Growth occurs in our reflection upon these interactions; if necessary, we can bring our reflections and concerns to a mentor. As we cultivate God-awareness, we begin to look for the gift in these encounters and we cultivate openness to life. Amma Theodora cautioned us to maintain balance in all aspects of our life, not being swayed toward any extreme.

2. Amma Theodora said, "Let us strive to enter by the narrow gate [see Matt 7:13–14]. Just as the trees, if they have not stood before the winter's storms cannot bear fruit, so it is with us; this present age is a storm, and it is only through many trials and temptations that we can obtain an inheritance in the kingdom of heaven."

Desert ascetics lived closely with nature, often at its mercy. This shaped much of their self-understanding and God-understanding. They lived intimately with the rhythm of harsh winters and fruitful springs.

God can use all our experiences to deepen our growth and transformation. A "winter's storm" is no indication that God has deserted us; rather, these seasons, as we reflectively respond to God's presence in the midst of them, become the test of our commitment to stand firm. They deepen our dedication to the inner journey and facilitate our transformation into the image of Christ. These seasons will come. If we watch attentively for their arrival and attend to our self-care, we will weather them just fine. The diversity of our liturgical seasons can be a helpful reminder that difficult times do come and that our God is still with us.

3. She also said, "It is good to practice contemplative quiet: a wise person leads a life of quiet contemplation. It's truly a great thing for an ascetic to practice contemplative quiet, especially those who are young. But—know this for a fact: if someone sets out to practice contemplative quiet, the Evil One quickly comes and weights down that person's soul: with acedia, with discouragement, with thoughts. He also weights down the body: with illnesses, with strained nerves, with weakness in the knees and in every part of the body, and dissolves the power of soul and body. As a result, I get weak and lack the energy to recite the synaxis.[19] But—if we're vigilant, all these things go out like a lamp.

"Here's an example: there was a certain ascetic. As soon as he began to recite the synaxis, he got chills and a fever and was bothered by a headache. So he said to himself, 'Look, I'm sick and I may die soon. So, before I die I'm going to get up and recite the synaxis.' He made every effort to resist the thought that he might die, and recited the synaxis. When the synaxis was almost done, his fever subsided. Once again the brother stood up to this thought that he might die: he offered the synaxis and defeated it."

What invasive conversations run through our minds, disturbing our attempts at prayer and inner quiet? Invasive thoughts or chatter, worries and anxieties can keep our spirits from restful peace that allows for the contemplative. We might listen to these disruptions or disturbances for their source, so that we can deal with them and find our way to inner peace again. Our goal is living from a contemplative stance.

The peace Amma Theodora calls us to has strength, substance, and weight. This peace is not a lack of turmoil but is rather a strength that moves toward life, integrating mind, body, soul, and spirit. Peace, or a contemplative presence, was a deeply held value among desert ascetics and monastics. They recognized that peace begins within each individual.

4. The same Amma Theodora said, "A devout person happened to be insulted by someone, and replied, 'I could say as much to you, but the commandment of God keeps my mouth shut.'"

Again she said this, "A Christian discussing the body with a Manichean said, 'Give the body discipline and you will see that the body is for the one who made it.'"

Amma Theodora did not say that the Christian pondered the meaning of the commandment and then decided it would be better not to speak; rather, the Christian had appropriated the commandment so completely that it shaped the Christian's behavior and attitude on the deepest level of his being.[20]

Amma Theodora warns her followers against letting bodily passions and desires, emotions, attitudes, and motives rule our lives. Passions, desires, and emotions are gifts from

God, but they were never meant to be out of balance, dominating, or controlling. Amma Theodora challenges us to bring our inner and outer world into congruence and harmony. This is interior freedom and simplicity.

5. The same Amma also used to say that the person who teaches should be a stranger to the love of power, alien to vanity and self-delusion, far from haughtiness and pride; the person who teaches should not seek out flattery, be blinded by gifts, conquered by the belly, or be ruled by anger. Instead, the person who teaches should be patient and even-tempered, courteous and forbearing, and as far as possible, completely humble. The one who teaches should be approved for the position, accommodating, prudent, and a lover of souls.

Amma Theodora insists that spiritual elders have a healthy relationship with power, recognizing the power dynamics of the spiritual mentoring relationship and placing responsibility on the elder for maintaining proper boundaries. If power is our motivation, we are a danger to those in our lives. Self-knowledge and humility are imperative here.

Amma Theodora teaches us that all authentic teachers have already begun the journey and teach only what they have already learned and cultivated in their personal lives. The maturity revealed in a balanced and disciplined life is essential.

6. She also said that neither asceticism, nor vigils nor all kinds of toil and suffering can save, only genuine humility can do that. There was an anchorite who was able to banish the demons, and asked them, "What makes you go away? Is it fasting?"

They replied, "We do not eat or drink."
"Is it vigils?" They replied, "We do not sleep."
"Is it separation from the world?" "We live in the deserts."
"What power sends you away then?"
They said, "Nothing can overcome us, but only humility."
"Do you see how humility means victory over demons?"

Humility is honest, accepting, and loving self-knowledge and self-awareness of ourselves as fully human, created and gifted by God, balanced with a keen awareness of God's grace and awesome presence in our life. Humility strengthens rather than diminishes our sense of self-worth. Humility is being grounded in reality.

Amma Theodora is using a literary tool—the characters of the demons—to reinforce her teachings on the inner journey. The end goal of the desert journey is complete and loving unity with God. Asceticism is a useful tool for growth into this unity. Asceticism is not a goal in itself. We must not confuse the process with its goal—unity with God.

7. Amma Theodora also said, "There was an ascetic who, because of the great number of personal temptations said, 'I will go away from here.' While putting sandals on, saw another ascetic who was also putting on sandals. This other ascetic said, 'Is it on my account that you are going away? Because I go before you wherever you are going.'"

Wherever we flee, we will only meet ourselves there. It is pointless to run away from difficult situations—we ourselves are part of the difficulty. Difficulties are an invitation to grow in self-awareness, in patience and inner strength, in humility and self-acceptance, and in God's immense and unconditional love. Difficulties teach us the real work of peacemaking.

Amma Theodora challenges her followers to be attentive to possible unpleasant motives in seeking a change in personal circumstances. In considering change, we must discern whether the sense of inner movement is away from difficulties or *toward* life. Quite often, this inner movement is not obvious.

> 8. The same Amma was asked about listening to others. "How can a person in general welcome what those in the world say and 'be with God alone,' as you say?"
>
> She said, "If you're having a meal and there's plenty to eat, you go ahead and eat with pleasure. In the same way, if you hear what those in the world are saying, keep your heart oriented toward God. By doing this, you will hear them, but not with pleasure and you won't be harmed at all."

In desert spirituality, one cultivates an intimacy with God that filters out anything harmful. Only those things that penetrate the heart are harmful.

Are we intentional about discerning to what we listen, our use of social media, what we watch on television, and what we read? We live in a very noisy society. What we consume *does* affect our minds and hearts. It takes focused and intentional work to cultivate the contemplative attitude and heart. We can be discerning about what touches and feeds our minds, hearts, and inner world.

> 9. An ascetic suffered bodily irritation and was infested with vermin. Now originally this ascetic had been rich. So the demons said, "How can

you bear to live like this, covered with vermin?"
But this ascetic, because of the greatness of soul,
was victorious over them.

In obvious and in subtle ways, our commitment to the
desert way will be questioned. Amma Theodora warned her
follower: we can meet someone special, experience a stirring of
our heart, or question our marriage commitment. When one
of our relationships—with a colleague or friend—becomes
difficult, other relationships begin to look attractive. We can
begin to look on our past with fond memories and romantic
illusions, believing that then must have been better than now.

Difficulty can seem like an indication that God has
deserted us. It is wise for us, in these times, to discern with
another the movement of our inner sense of God's call in our
life and to stand firm in our commitments. Greatness of soul
or spiritual maturity deepens when we choose to remain true.

10. Another of the old ascetics questioned Amma
Theodora saying, "At the resurrection of the
dead, how shall we rise?" She said, "As pledge,
example, and as prototype we have him who
died for us and is risen, Christ our God."

Amma Theodora held a firm, steadfast hope and trust in
the resurrection. In her oneness of spirit with God, she knew
deeply that ultimate unity with God would be experienced
only in our resurrection after death. With other desert ascetics
and monastics, death—and hence resurrection—was the
focus kept ever before their eyes.

The desert way cultivated an awareness of the small
glimpses of resurrection already present and a hope grounded
in the resurrection.

Chapter Four

BRIGHT STARS IN THE DESERT SKY

Lesser-Known Desert Mothers

The following, arranged in alphabetical order by name, are the stories of ammas whose Sayings did not survive the course of history. Seeking solitude in city or desert, each woman had a unique story, except for the shared intense search for God.

ALEXANDRA

Alexandria in Egypt was a major port established where the Nile meets the Mediterranean Sea. There was an important Christian community there, and it was a growing intellectual center. One of the earliest schools of theology was located in this city.

Alexandra was a beautiful, young fourth-century woman who fled the unwanted advances of a young man, left the city of Alexandria, and shut herself up in a mausoleum. She received food and supplies through a window from a woman friend. Alexandra maintained strict privacy through the remaining ten or twelve years of her life, keeping a curtain at her window so that no one ever saw her face-to-face again.

Melania the Elder sought a visit with Alexandra. When Melania asked Alexandra how she persevered through the harsh conditions and the difficult inner journey, she replied,

> From early dawn to the ninth hour I weave linen, and recite the Psalms and pray; and during the rest of the day I commemorate in my heart the holy fathers, and I revolve in my thoughts the histories of all the Prophets and Apostles, and Martyrs; and during the remaining hours I work with my hands and eat my bread, and by means of these things I am comforted whilst I await the end of my life in good hope.[1]

Despite her strict privacy, Alexandra developed a reputation among Christians for her wise advice and spiritual direction. Her feast day is February 14.

THE ANONYMOUS MAIDEN

A young and reportedly beautiful woman lived alone in her home in Alexandria, Egypt. In 355 CE during the reign of Emperor Constantius II, Athanasius,[2] bishop of Alexandria, was again falsely accused before the emperor by his Arian detractors. As officers came to arrest him, he fled rather than allow himself to be judged by a corrupt court. Not wanting to involve his family or fellow clergy, Athanasius—led by the Holy Spirit—went to the home of this young ascetic, knowing it was the last place anyone would expect to find him. This was because people expected him to never be alone with a woman, outside a family member, as his reputation would be tarnished. She supported him and borrowed books for his use. She hid and protected him for six years, until the death of the emperor in 361 CE. Apparently, her youth and beauty left her above suspicion.

ASELLA

From the earliest days of the Jesus movement, Rome attracted active and dedicated groups of women who were committed to prayer, service to the marginalized, and the study of scripture. They soon developed into urban monastic communities. Often attached to one of these communities would be a solitary. Asella was one of the earliest.

Born around 334 CE, Asella and her sister Marcella were members of a noble and wealthy Roman family.[3] Jerome, Athanasius of Alexandria, and the historian Palladius were among her friends and mentors. Asella consecrated herself to God when she was ten years of age.[4] At twelve she chose—with some initial family resistance—to live the life of a solitary ascetic. Jerome describes her life in her family's home in Rome:

> Enclosed in the narrow confines of a single cell, she enjoyed the wide pastures of paradise. The same patch of earth existed as her place both of prayer and of rest. Fasting was her recreation and hunger her refreshment. If she took food, it was not from love of eating but from human exhaustion, and the bread, salt, and cold water to which she restricted herself sharpened more than appeased her appetite.[5]

Asella gave all her possessions away and dressed only in dark clothing. Jerome mentions her sale of a gold necklace in a lamprey pattern with bars of gold linked together to form a flexible chain. The money was given to the poor.

Asella lived in silence and privacy, appearing discreetly in public only when she attended the Church of the Holy Martyrs. She rarely saw her family, including her sister Marcella, although her cell was in the family compound. She fasted several days a week and framed her day in a regular schedule of prayer and psalmody. The few who had contact with her, including Jerome and Palladius, remarked at her cheerful, gentle, and pleasant disposition. Jerome tells us,

> She is equally pleasant in her serious moods and serious in her pleasant moods. She is equally solemn in her laughter and charming in her sadness. Her face is pale enough to indicate continence but not ostentatiously to display austerity. Her speech is silence and her silence speech.[6]

In later years, her family compound became a monastery with a portion dedicated to hospitality and to receiving and instructing converts. Asella died between 405 and 408. Her feast day is December 6.

ATHANASIA OF ANTIOCH AND EGYPT

Antioch was an inland city in present-day Syria, located at a major crossroad for traffic from Asia Minor, especially for Roman troop movement. Antioch rivaled Alexandria as a growing intellectual center and for its important contributions to theology.

Athanasia and her husband, Andronicus, were prosperous silver merchants who lived in Antioch with their two children. They were generous believers and gave a third of their wealth away to the poor. Both their children died at the age of twelve. Athanasia was inconsolable. She mourned deeply, spending most of her time at the church of Saint Julian the Martyr. While in intense prayer, Athanasia saw a vision of Saint Julian that irrevocably changed their lives.

Athanasia and Andronicus decided to sell all they owned, giving all their wealth to hospitals and monastic communities.

They journeyed to Jerusalem to visit the holy places, and then to Egypt to consult with Abba Daniel. They decided that Athanasia would begin her desert journey by joining a monastic community in Tabennisi while Andronicus stayed with Abba Daniel.

Twelve years later, Athanasia was journeying to Jerusalem on pilgrimage when she encountered her husband. Athanasia recognized her husband, but Andronicus did not recognize his wife. They agreed to journey together, maintaining total silence as if each was alone.

Upon return to the desert region outside Alexandria, the two decided to share a cave together, continuing to live in deep silence. They lived this eremitical life for twelve years, until the death of Athanasia. Many of the desert dwellers and monastics in the area attended her funeral. Their feast day is celebrated on October 9.

ATHANASIA OF CONSTANTINOPLE

Athanasia was an independently wealthy married woman. After developing a friendship with Matrona and her monastic community, Athanasia decided she wanted to give all her wealth to Matrona and join them. Matrona initially refused this request, reminding Athanasia that she was still young (eighteen) and lacked her husband's consent. Matrona encouraged her to begin her training for the ascetic life by living simply and chastely, devoting several times each day to prayer.

Athanasia went to live on one of her farms and sought an appropriate way to separate from her extravagant and intemperate husband. Soon she discovered that he had spent all his fortune and that he had stolen some of her cash while she was at her farm. This was sufficient grounds for a divorce. Athanasia won her freedom,[7] took most of her wealth with her, and joined Matrona's community.

Athanasia's wealth was used to enlarge the hermitage and construct a church for the community. Another large portion was sent to needy monasteries in Jerusalem. The remainder was distributed among the poor. Athanasia remained with this community until her death in 373 CE. Her feast day is May 2.

CAESARIA THE PATRICIAN

Samosata was an ancient city located on the Euphrates River in northern Syria. It held some importance to the Roman military after its capture in 72 CE.

A colleague of John of Ephesus[8] and Severus of Antioch, Caesaria the Patrician was an early sixth-century woman of prominence from Samosata, whose husband was of imperial descent. After years of marriage, Caesaria sought to establish a monastic and solitary life for herself,[9] accepted the clothing of an ascetic, and intensified her prayer life. She was known for her faithful presence at the Divine Office, her dedication to intercessory prayer, and her love of silence and solitude.

Like many of her social class who underwent conversions, Caesaria renounced her royal lifestyle. She fasted stringently, eating only every other day, and slept on the ground. She was admonished to greater moderation but steadfastly chose more extreme asceticism, desiring to break fully from her former life.

Caesaria was well educated, both in scripture and in the writings of early church leaders. Her personal library contained over seven hundred volumes that she had read with such understanding that she could converse energetically with John of Ephesus. She was particularly interested in understanding the process of discernment. This is especially notable, as Caesaria lived through some of the church's doctrinal turmoil.[10]

Caesaria sought to leave the monastic community she founded and move deeper into the desert with two companions. John of Ephesus talked her out of this, partly due to her old age and fragile health, and partly due to her importance to the local community.

Caesaria established two monastic communities, one for women and one for men, in the desert near Alexandria, and endowed them with a gold mine. Refusing to serve as abbess, she appointed Cosmiana to this position. Caesaria lived the monastic life for fifteen years, until her death in 556 CE.

BLESSED WOMAN CANDIDA

Candida was the daughter of General Trajan. Modeling her life on the example of Deaconess Olympias of Constantinople, Candida gave financial support to the churches and clergy. She instructed her daughter in the ascetic life and eventually gave her to a monastery. After deciding to join a monastery herself, Candida gave away all her wealth to the poor and needy.

Following the common example of monastics, Candida spent her nights in prayer while grinding corn and baking bread for the Offering. She valued fasting and ate a near-vegetarian diet of only fish and vegetables with oil. Her spirituality was focused on a hope-filled waiting for the resurrection.

AMMA CERONA

Cerona was born in Cornillan, near Beziers in Gaul, present-day France. Cerona and her brother were adult converts who received instruction in the Christian faith from the bishop of Bordeaux. In 440 CE, she traveled north to the

Diocese of Seez and built a small cell in the forest near Mortagne near Mont Romigny. Cerona balanced times of solitude with travel in her immediate area, seeking the conversion of the inhabitants.

Cerona eventually established the region's first monastery for women. She also built several oratories, one on a spot where pre-Christian funeral rites had been conducted. Cerona served as leader to this monastic community but maintained her solitary cell. She died in 490 CE, and her feast day was celebrated on November 16 and February 3.

DOMNINA

Theodoret of Cyrrhus tells us that Domnina was an ascetic in the southern region of Syria. She set up a small hut in the garden of her mother's home to maintain solitude and was supported by her family. She continued a strong connection with the local church, attending morning and evening prayer each day. She was sought out for spiritual direction. Domnina wore rough and uncomfortable garments made of haircloth, with a hood that covered her face. She lived on a simple vegetarian diet. Domnina died around 460 CE, and her feast is celebrated on March 1.

ERMELINDA

A sixth-century hermit, Ermelinda was born into a noble family near Louvain in present-day Belgium. Her family owned extensive lands in northern France, and Ermelinda spent portions of her childhood on different estates. She began to live the ascetic life in her parents' home.

When Ermelinda chose to become a hermit, her parents gave her a neighboring estate. She soon decided that she could not focus solely on her pursuit of God with her family nearby. Moving near the village of Bevec, Ermelinda lived as a virtual unknown in a small, simple hut and entered the village only to attend the Divine Office.

When she began to attract the attention of villagers, Ermelinda moved to the Diocese of Mechlin (Belgium) and continued to live the life of a hermit. It is here that she spent the remainder of her life. Her feast day is October 29.

EUGENIA OF ALEXANDRIA

The story of Eugenia evolved into a fantastic martyr-legend. However, the mosaic was formed from historical pieces of an earlier woman.

Eugenia was the daughter of Philip, proconsul of Egypt under Commodus from 180 to 192 CE. She was raised in a pagan Roman family but privately began to follow the Christian way. Eugenia rejected an arranged marriage to Aquilinus, a man of high standing but not a follower of the Way. Before another suitable marriage could be arranged, Eugenia and two of her fellow students met a monastic community of men and decided to join.

Disguised as a man, Eugenia entered the community and quietly began to live the monastic life. Eventually elected abbot, she reluctantly accepted the office and made a little cell for herself by the side of the monastery door, that she might remain in it continually. She protected her desire for silence and solitude while serving as spiritual elder for the brethren.

It is recorded that Eugenia was martyred in Rome around 257 CE, during the reign of Valerian and Gallienus.[11] Her feast day is December 25 in the West and December 24 in the East.

EUPHRASIA THE ELDER AND EUPHRASIA THE YOUNGER

Euphrasia was a young widow with a daughter, also named Euphrasia. When she became the unintentional cause of a dispute between Emperor Theodosius and his wife, Euphrasia took her daughter and moved to Egypt, where she owned some estates. She began to visit churches and monasteries, leaving sizeable donations behind.

Eventually Euphrasia visited a women's monastery deep in the Theban desert and decided she and her daughter would join them. This community of 130 ascetics followed a regular schedule of fasting and abstinence from wine, wore hairshirts, slept on hair mats, and refused to bathe. They spent their time in intense prayer. Euphrasia died at this monastery when her daughter was around five years old. The monastic community raised her daughter.

Young Euphrasia's family had betrothed her to a suitor despite her distance from the royal court. When Euphrasia was of marriageable age, her betrothed asked Emperor Theodosius to see that the marriage proceeded as contracted. The younger Euphrasia wrote the emperor of her desire to remain with her monastic community and asked him to distribute her wealth to the churches and the poor, and for the care of orphans.

Euphrasia lived a contented life in the desert. She developed a close friendship with another noblewoman named Julia. Julia taught Euphrasia to read, sing, and pray. They baked the community bread together and shared all their deepest struggles and joys. Euphrasia lived to around thirty years of age, and then died of a fever. Her feast day is March 13.

EUPHROSYNE OF ALEXANDRIA

Euphrosyne (meaning "good cheer") was born in Alexandria in 410 CE to a wealthy and prominent family. Euphrosyne was given an education, including the scriptures, and became known for her love of learning and her growth in wisdom. As she was their only child, her parents arranged for an advantageous marriage.

When Euphrosyne was eighteen years old, she went with her father, Paphnutius, on retreat to a monastery for men for three days of intense prayer. The abbot also privately instructed her. Euphrosyne fell in love with the monastic life. She sought the help of a wandering ascetic as well as a monastic hermit to prepare for a life of monastic observance.

When her father left her at home to go on another retreat, she took the opportunity to slip away. A hermit from Scete shaved her head, gave her a monastic robe, prayed with her, and departed. She quickly decided not to join any women's community for fear her father would find her; so she changed into men's clothing, took five hundred dinars, and went to join the men's community that she and her father had visited. Euphrosyne told the porter that she was a eunuch from the palace, named Esmeraldus. The abbot placed Euphrosyne in training under Agapius, one of the elders of the community.

Dissension arose in the community over Euphrosyne's beauty, and the abbot ordered her into seclusion. She moved deeper into the desert to a more solitary cell and began to recite services alone rather than join the monastic community for prayers. Euphrosyne quickly grew to love the intense solitude and ceased having contact with anyone other than the abbot and Father Agapios, her elder and mentor.

Euphrosyne's grieving father sought out the assistance of the abbot in the search for his "abducted" daughter. The abbot assisted, unaware that Euphrosyne was in his community. Eventually, Paphnutius began coming to the monastery for solace from his grief, and the abbot sent him to Euphrosyne for comfort and spiritual direction. Euphrosyne met him, keeping her face covered with a veil and never revealing her identity. Paphnutius returned several times, as they had drawn close from their personal sharing.

Euphrosyne lived near this monastic community for thirty-eight years, with no one discovering that she was a woman. In the last year of her life, Paphnutius again visited on retreat and met with Euphrosyne for direction. Aware that she was dying, Euphrosyne revealed her identity to her father, and there was a final reconciliation.

At her request, Paphnutius distributed the family wealth to the poor, hospitals, and prisons, and to the monastery. The monastic community buried her, and her tomb quickly became a place of prayer with miracles attributed to her. Paphnutius moved into Euphrosyne's cave and dwelt there for ten years, until his own death.

An early version of her Life was written in iambic pentameter. Saint Symeon the Translator wrote her Life in prose.[12] Euphrosyne's feast is celebrated on September 25.

FEBRONIA OF SEBAPTE

While accounts of the passion[13] and death of Febronia, much like those of Jesus, grew and became more elaborate over time, at the core is a historical woman. Uniquely, the core of her story was written by a fellow nun named Thomais. In subsequent centuries, several churches and monasteries were named in her honor.

Born in 284 CE in Sebapte, Febronia was raised in a community of ascetics near Nisibis (Mesopotamia). She was well educated, surpassing many in the community in wisdom.

She was one of the lectors who proclaimed the scriptures before the community and guests. She became good friends with the widow Hieria, a senator's widow who converted to Christianity after hearing Febronia read and explain Sacred Scripture.

During one of Emperor Diocletian's persecutions, Febronia was brought before the authorities for trial. Due to her beauty, Selenos, the Roman authority in charge of persecutions in the area, offered her an arranged marriage to his nephew, Lysimachus, if she would also renounce her faith. She refused. She countered every charge and debated Selenos, speaking from her own authority. She refused to back down and, condemned to death, was tortured and executed. Her feast days are June 25 in the West and February 12 in the East.

FLORENCE OF POITIERS

During one of the early christological controversies called Arianism, the Roman emperor intervened and tried to coerce all bishops to embrace his chosen position. All bishops who refused were banished. The personal witness of Saint Hilary of Poitiers—who sided with the orthodox position— converted Florence to Christianity during his exile in Phrygia. Florence and Hilary returned together to Poitiers in 360 CE. She lived in a cell near Poitiers under the guidance of the recluse Amma Triaise until her death in 367 CE. Her feast day is December 1.

FRACLA, POSENNA, AND PROMPTA

Fracla, Posenna, and Prompta, who lived at the end of the fifth century, were three Irish sisters who went on a pilgrimage to northern Gaul with their seven sisters and brothers. The sisters settled on the banks of the Marne River near Rheims to live as hermits, each in a separate cell. Their feast day is January 3.

BLESSED WOMAN GELASIA

Gelasia was the daughter of a tribune, who followed Candida into the monastic life. Palladius tells us, "Her virtue is said to be such that the sun never set on her anger, not even at manservant or handmaid."[14]

HILARIA

We know of Hilaria from an apocryphal[15] story that calls her the older daughter of the Emperor Zeno (474–91 CE). As befitting their royal background, Hilaria and her sister were well educated and memorized the psalms.

Hilaria was deeply influenced by the martyrdom of the forty-nine fathers of Scete and decided to become a monastic herself. She fled her home disguised as a man and sailed to Alexandria. At the church of the Holy Mar Marcus, Hilaria met a deacon named Theodorus, who escorted her to Scete to see Abba Banfu (Pambo). Abba Pambo was reluctant to take Hilaria, due to her obvious upper-class background. When Hilaria's determination and quick wit became obvious, Abba Pambo, believing she was a young man, accepted her as a disciple and began to train her in the desert way. Hilaria was known in the region as Hilary the Eunuch, which explained her lack of a beard.

Hilaria's younger sister went on pilgrimage to Scete seeking a cure from a serious illness. Abba Pambo ordered Hilaria to host the princess in her cell. Hilaria prayed for her day and night until the princess had a full recovery. The princess returned home amazed, as much at the deep love she experienced from this unknown monk as at her cure.

The Emperor Zeno, suffering from heart trouble, ordered the unknown monk to come to him at the royal court in Constantinople. Hilaria agreed only because Abba Pambo ordered her. After eliciting a vow of silence, Hilaria revealed her identity to her father and prayed for his healing. The emperor endowed the monks of Scete in thanksgiving both for the younger princess's healing and for his reconciliation with Hilaria.

BLESSED WOMAN JULIANA

Following the election of the very learned Firmilian as bishop in 230 CE, Caesarea, in Cappadocia, evolved into an important theological center. Juliana, a resident of Caesarea, was an erudite and well-educated woman of prominence.

During the persecution against Egyptian Christians in 235 CE, Origen, a leading theologian, fled Alexandria.[16] Juliana hid him in her home for two years and supported him financially.[17] She had lived a life of solitude in her own home, and when she invited Origen to live with her as a brother, no scandal arose because her reputation was above suspicion.

Juliana is held up as an example of someone who makes every experience an opportunity for learning. She is honored in the Orthodox[18] tradition for her capacities as a teacher of Sacred Scripture. She owned books and was a woman of understanding. Palladius discovered the following words in an old book of verse, written in Origen's own hand: "I found this book among the things of Juliana the virgin in Caesarea when I was hidden by her. She used to say that she had it from Symmachus himself, the translator of the Jews."[19]

MANNA OF FONTENET

Living in the fourth century, Manna was the daughter of Sigmar and Liutrude. Manna (sometimes "Menna") was baptized and instructed in the household of the bishop of Chalons in Gaul, present-day France. She refused to marry a non-Christian nobleman and took the veil of an ascetic.

At the death of her parents, their wealth was divided among their children. Soon, Manna and her siblings dispersed because of the persecutions under Julian the Apostate.[20] She and her maid fled to the forests of Fontenet and built a hermitage near a spring. She remained in her hermitage the rest of her life. The area eventually became known as *Le Gue de Sainte Manne*. Her feast day is October 3.

MARANA AND CYRA

Theodoret of Cyrrhus tells us of two noblewomen who founded a small monastery in Beroea (Syria). Around 398 CE, Marana and Cyra purchased a roofless building on the outskirts of this city. They walled up the door with clay and stone. They also built a separate dwelling for the women who joined them.

Marana and Cyra served as ammas to this community while living in seclusion and silence. Marana gave outsiders spiritual counsel only during the season of Pentecost. For the remainder of the year, she and her sister spoke only with their community. As was common in Syrian asceticism, Marana and Cyra practiced mortification of the flesh: they wore iron chains daily and went on long fasts. Several times the bishop asked them to moderate their asceticism, to no avail.

Marana and Cyra lived the ascetical life for forty-two years, leaving their enclosure only twice: to go on pilgrimage to Aelia and to the shrine of Saint Thecla at Isauria.

BLESSED MARIA THE HARP PLAYER

Cyril of Scythopolis tells us Maria was a liturgical musician.[21] She served as a harp player and cantor in the Holy Church of the Resurrection of Christ in Jerusalem. Sensing a call to a life of deep prayer and solitude, Maria moved into the desert near Sousakim in the region of the Dead Sea. Maria filled her clay vessel at the pool of Siloam, took a basket of soaked legumes (a common, simple desert food), and moved with her harp into a cave that served as her hermitage for eighteen years. Travelers walking in this region would hear Maria playing her harp but would not know where it came from.

Abba John and Abba Parammon were journeying to the anchorite Abba Cyriacus when they encountered a desert anchorite who was unfamiliar to them. Drawing near, deep in prayer, lest they encounter an evil spirit, they discovered a woman living in an underground cave. Maria was reluctant to speak to them, hesitant to reveal either her identity or her location to the public. Maria told them her story: she had never left her cave nor spoken to anyone until encountering them, and her pitcher of water and basket of legumes never ran out.

On their way back to their own monastery at Chariton, John and Parammon discovered Maria's corpse and buried her in her own cave. The entrance was sealed with stones. Her feast day is September 29.

BLESSED WOMAN MARINA

Marina,[22] a fifth-century woman, was raised and educated by her father, Eugenios.[23] When she reached marriageable age, Eugenios announced his intention of giving all his wealth to her and becoming a desert ascetic. Marina refused to be left behind and insisted on following her father into the ascetic life.

They decided that Marina would crop her hair short, wear men's clothing, and change her name to the masculine "Marinos" in order to enter the same monastery as her father. Eugenios gave all their wealth away, and they went to join the community.

Marina embraced the monastic observance faithfully. She became known for her obedience, humility, and great devotion to prayer. No one suspected Marina was a woman but assumed she was a eunuch. She lived with her father in his cave until his death, after which her reputation for hard work and spiritual maturity continued to grow.

One day, the abbot sent Marina off with three other monks to visit other monasteries and conduct business. On their journey, the monks spent the night at an inn they frequently used. While they were there, a soldier seduced the innkeeper's daughter and suggested that if she became pregnant, she should accuse Marina.

The innkeeper's daughter claimed that Marina had seduced her and fathered her child. Not revealing her identity, Marina accepted this accusation and begged for forgiveness. The abbot expelled Marina, who then lived right outside the monastery gates. When the baby boy was brought to Marina, she accepted him without protest.

Marina and the child lived outside the monastery gate for four years. She continually requested readmittance and "confessed her sin of fornication to all who passed by." The monastic community was deeply moved by Marina's continual requests to reenter, and eventually she was allowed to return to the monastery with the child. Marina accepted the lowest rank in the community and resumed her life of simplicity and austerity. Only at her death did the community discover that she was a woman. The abbot grieved for his treatment of Marina, realizing that his judgment was based on mere external appearances.

Her feast days are June 18 in the West and February 12 in the East.

MARY THE ANCHORITE

John of Ephesus tells us that Mary was the daughter of a noble family. While still quite young, she met a holy man from a neighboring town. She decided to live as he did and rejected marriage. Her parents, upon discovering her intent, began wedding preparations for fear they would lose the rich man to whom she was betrothed.

Mary left home, took the habit, and cropped her hair in the manner of ascetics. She joined a monastic community and later lived as a desert ascetic for thirty years, in imitation of the holy old man. She focused her spiritual journey on the attainment of interior freedom. She was renowned for the power of her prayer.

Mary was involved for fifteen years in the Monophysite controversy. She hosted, financially supported, and defended many of its more outspoken adherents. She treated this controversy as a holy war and was seen as a hero in the local church.

MARY AND EUPHEMIA, TWO HOLY SISTERS CALLED DAUGHTERS OF THE GAZELLE

Mary the Pilgrim[24] was an urban hermit who resided in the region of Tella d-Mauzlath in southeastern Turkey. She lived a life of quiet, fasting, recitation of the Divine Office, continual prayer, and profound generosity. Wandering and continuous pilgrimage was a form of asceticism that kept Mary from being attached to any place and allowed her to focus on intense prayer. Holy sites were her usual destinations.

Mary made an extended pilgrimage to Jerusalem in order to pray at the holy places. When she arrived at Golgotha, she was lifted up in ecstasy and remained in deep prayer for three days and three nights. She was so moved by this experience that she remained in Jerusalem for three years, living among the very poor in churches and on the street, and maintaining strict silence. Golgotha was her favored place of solitude and prayer.

Pilgrims from the East recognized Mary as the woman of great honor from Tella and began to spread her story. Mary, appalled at being recognized and having people pay her homage, fled Jerusalem and returned to Tella. She returned each year to Golgotha on pilgrimage, and many miracles occurred because of her presence.

Euphemia, her younger sister, had been married as a young woman and also lived in southeastern Turkey. When she was widowed, she and her daughter, Maria, turned their home in Amida into a hermitage. They wore religious garb, prayed the Divine Office, and relieved the afflicted.

Euphemia and Maria decided to support themselves by the work of their own hands, living on half their earnings and using the remainder to provide cooked food, bread, and wine for the poor, sick, and those in prison. Euphemia sought out the marginalized in order to talk and pray with them as well as meet their needs. She treated each as a unique individual. Euphemia became known as "our consolation and our visitor."

During a period of turmoil within the church over doctrine, Euphemia opened her house to those driven from their monasteries and homes. As the numbers seeking her hospitality grew, she rented a larger home and turned it into a monastery. Her daughter remained secluded in silence. Euphemia accepted the generosity of the believing community to support those seeking her help while continuing to support herself by the work of her own hands.

After thirty years of dedicated work, Euphemia was arrested and imprisoned for her hospitality to exiles.[25] Eventually she was banished from the city. Euphemia and Maria went to join Mary on pilgrimage to Jerusalem. After five years, Euphemia attempted a quiet return to her city but was discovered. As she was preparing to depart again, Euphemia fell seriously ill. As she lay dying, her final parting words were to Maria:

> My daughter, take comfort in Christ and guard yourself in purity.…I am entrusting you to the child of our blessed lady Mary, and to the Holy One herself, that by her prayers you may be guarded, and become a temple of the dwelling of the Holy Spirit of God.[26]

MASTRIDIA OF JERUSALEM

Mastridia lived a quiet ascetical life in Jerusalem. She was known for her gentleness, modesty of spirit, and compassionate love for her neighbors. Due to her deep wisdom and understanding of the interior life, she was referred to as a "female man of God."

In order to seek more intense solitude and union with God, Mastridia took some soaked beans in a basket, moved to the desert mountains, and embraced the hermit life for seventeen years.

Mastridia died around 580 CE. Her feast day is February 7.

MATRONA OF PERGE

Born around 425 CE in Perge, Matrona[27] was married to Domitianus and was the mother of a daughter named

Theodote (meaning "given by God"). Conventional upper-class life in Constantinople left Matrona dissatisfied, and she yearned for change. She began to spend days and nights attending prayer services.

Soon she found mentors in two urban ascetics, Eugenia and Susanna. In order to follow their lifestyles, Matrona cropped her hair short and dressed in men's clothing. Seeking to escape her husband, she entered the men's monastery of Basianus in Constantinople and took the name of Babylas. Susanna took responsibility for raising Matrona's daughter.

When her identity was discovered and her husband demanded her return, Abbot Basianus arranged to send her to a women's monastery near Emesa in Syria. Matrona became known for her powerful prayer life and effectiveness in praying for the healing of others.

Matrona finally settled as a desert ascetic in an abandoned pagan temple in the desert near Beirut. Her fame as a spiritual director and teacher grew, and many came to spend time with her there. There were many conversions, especially of women. Disciples, including a woman named Sophrone and a former priestess, began to join her and share her life in the desert.

Around 457 CE, after the death of her husband, Matrona returned to Constantinople with eight of her followers to establish a monastery. They bought an estate near the Church of Saint Laurentius and began their monastic observance. They wore male monastic garb openly. The community grew large and prosperous and was renowned as a place of prayer, healing, and learning. Women of all social classes, including the very poor, were welcomed as members and as visitors.

Matrona was a staunch supporter of the Council of Chalcedon (451 CE), but Emperor Anastasios I favored the Monophysites. The emperor tried to force her to publicly support his position, but Matrona refused and he eventually backed down.

Matrona was abbess until her death in 524 CE at the age of 100. Her feast is November 9.

MONEGUND, RECLUSE OF TOURS

After the death of her two daughters, Monegund[28] chose to live alone on her family estate in Chartres, present-day France. She lived in a spacious cell with a fireplace and a window. Monegund, rejecting a comfortable bed with goose down covers, slept on a mat of woven rushes. In order to protect Monegund's solitude, a maid brought her water and other basic necessities.

Monegund was dedicated to a life of intercessory prayer and fasting. Gregory of Tours said that she would bake soda bread and distribute it to the poor. She cultivated a large garden that included healing herbs. The many poor who came to her for food also began to seek physical healing. Her prayer for their healing often included herbal mixtures and massage.

Monegund, like many in her region, yearned to live near the shrine of Saint Martin of Tours; she was also concerned that those seeking her help too often disrupted her day. Monegund moved to Tours and found a cell to live in. Soon her husband and friends came to retrieve her and forcibly brought her home to Chartres.

Again slipping away to Tours, Monegund began to mentor a group of other women in the solitary life. As her death drew near, she blessed oil and salt so that her healing ministry could continue.

Monegund died in 570 CE. The group of women eventually developed into the monastery of Saint Pierre-le-Puellier. Her feast day is July 2.

NYMPHODORA, MENODORA, AND METRODORA

Nymphodora, Menodora, and Metrodora[29] were sisters who lived as recluses in a *tumulus*, a domelike mound formed in hardened lava, near the hot springs of Pythiis in Bithynia in northwestern Asia Minor. They were spiritual elders and mentors to many and were known for their powerful healing prayer ministry. All three were eventually martyred during the persecutions of Diocletian and Maximian around 304 CE for refusing to make sacrifices to the emperor's favorite pagan gods. Their feast day is September 10.

PAËSIA

Paësia[30] was a generous, compassionate believer in fourth-century Egypt. When she was orphaned, she turned her home into a hospice for desert dwellers. When her resources were exhausted, some men convinced her to become a courtesan.

John the Dwarf soon learned of her situation, and remembering her unwavering generosity toward others, went to see her. He went into her chamber and sat beside her on the bed. Looking into her eyes, he asked, "What have you got against Jesus that you behave like this?" and began weeping. Paësia's heart began to stir with grief. She asked, "Is it possible to repent?" And he replied, "Yes." She responded, "Then take me where you wish." When they finished speaking, she followed John into the desert region of Scete. John the Dwarf made a little pillow in the sand for each of them, marking each with a cross, and they went to sleep. Waking up in the middle of the night, he saw a shining path reaching from heaven and he saw angels bearing away her soul. He saw she was dead. Praying, he heard, "One single hour of repentance has brought her more than the penances of many who continue without showing such fervor of repentance."

PHOTINA

Photina was the sole survivor of a fourth-century shipwreck in the Mediterranean Sea. The recluse Martinian, the sole resident of a small and barren island, saved her but soon left her alone on the island.

Martinian's regular contact, a boatman, returned two months later and found Photina alone on this island. Choosing to live as a recluse, she made arrangements to spin wool in return for food and water. The boatman also provided Photina with a monk's garb.

Photina remained alone on this island as a hermit for six years. She died at the age of thirty-one in 400 CE. The boatman and wife found her dead and made arrangements for her burial at Caesaria. Her feast day is February 13.

AMMA PIAMON

Near a small village on the banks of the Upper Nile, Piamon and her mother lived a life of simplicity and austerity. Piamon spent her nights in vigil, a common practice among ascetics, who often strove to cultivate the ability to spend the night in constant prayer in anticipation of Christ's return at dawn. She ate every other evening and spun flax for linen.

Piamon was renowned for her gift of prophecy and her powers of intercessory prayer. When her village was under threat of attack by a neighboring city over water rights, Piamon's help was sought. Her neighbors were afraid to confront their enemy and were unwilling to defend themselves. They looked to her to settle the dispute or defend the town on their behalf.

Piamon spent the night in intense prayer, and through her intercession, the threat was averted, and peace made. Her feast day is March 3.

PUSINNA OF BANSION

Pusinna was the well-educated daughter of rich Christians. She made her consecration before Alpina, bishop of Chalons-sur-Marne (d. 461 CE). She gave all she possessed to the poor and spent her days in prayer and fasting. Eventually she retired to a solitary cell in the village of Bansion, near Corbie. Pusinna died in the latter part of the fifth century and was buried at Bansion.

ROMANA OF TODI

Todi is a lovely town built on the side and at the pinnacle of Mount Soracte in the Tuscany region of Italy. The slopes of Mount Soracte have natural caves. Romana was a young woman who lived in one of these caves, maintaining intense solitude until her death in 324 CE. Two local priests knew of her presence. Her feast day is February 23.

HOLY SHIRIN, BLESSED AMONG WOMEN

Shirin was a sixth-century solitary ascetic who lived in the village of Halmon, in present-day northern Iraq. John of Ephesus and the Syrian monastic writer Martyrios (also known as Sahdona) both knew Shirin, and Martyrios's mother became one of her followers.

Shirin cultivated a powerful prayer life, praying the Divine Office and maintaining continuous prayer. She was known for her ministry of intercessory prayer, and villagers believed she had "power over Satan." She dedicated time each day to studying scripture, theology, and monastic writings.

Shirin lived a simple life of hardship. Her ascetic life was without guile, and she maintained integrity and authenticity in her inner journey. People experienced her as serene, gentle, simple, and filled with compassionate love. Her home was open to all, and she became known for her hospitality.

Shirin was a spiritual director to monastics as well as lay people. She inspired others to a zealous observance of their faith life, more by example than words. Abbots sought her counsel and looked to her as a spiritual elder.

She lived into her eighties.

SOSIANA

Sosiana had enjoyed a long and happy married life to her husband, John, with whom she served as chamberlain to Caesaria the Patrician. Upon John's death, Sosiana decided to join Caesaria's monastic community. Sosiana surrendered all of her possessions and committed herself to trust God for her needs.

She gave John of Ephesus all of her husband's and her own expensive clothing, silk cloth, and embroidery to be made into altar cloths. She also gave up many pounds of silver to be made into chalices and patens. John distributed these during his mission of 542 CE to the churches and monasteries he had founded in Asia.

Sosiana lived in Caesaria's community until she died quietly and quickly from an illness.

BLESSED HERMIT SUSAN

John of Ephesus tells us "this woman, then, holy and manly in Christ...astonished me by her appearance, words, and strength in God."[31] Susan was from a fifth-century noble family of Persian Arzanene near the Tigris River. From early childhood, she was known for her sensibility, modesty, and devotion.

At an early age Susan dreamt of praying at the holy shrines, and especially of going to Jerusalem. Her parents refused because she was only eight years old.[32] She began to pray earnestly that God would open doors for her to travel. Finally, trusting in God's protection, Susan ran away from home.

Susan joined a caravan of women and men traveling to Jerusalem. When the caravan was ready to return, Susan refused to join them. Instead she joined a monastery of women situated between Ascalon and Gaza. She lived the common life of prayer and manual labor.

After ten years, the monastery fell under persecution by followers of the teachings of the Council of Chalcedon. Rather than submit, Susan left for the desert beyond Alexandria. Eventually, five other nuns from her community joined her there. They moved deeper into the desert near the monastery of Mar Menas, two miles from the village of Mendis. The women moved into an old watchtower, continuing their common life.

Wanting to live the life of a solitary and hermit, Susan would go out wandering and praying in the desert. One day she discovered an underground cave. Without returning for provisions, she moved in. Her community soon went looking for her and eventually found her. Susan refused to leave her cave, determined to continue growing in silence and inner strength. At the women's continued urging to return with them, Susan told them, "My sisters, leave me alone. I am with you for all time; but because the Lord prepared this place for me, so that I might easily live in quietude here, go and stay in peace."[33] They finally agreed to leave Susan to her solitude if she would accept a Sunday offering of dried bread and a pitcher of water.

This continued for three years. Word of her reputation began to spread around the region of Alexandria and the villages of Libya. People came to visit her. An old man named Maro with about ten disciples from a community in Palestine had been wandering during the persecutions. Upon hearing of the whereabouts of these women and especially of the growing reputation of Susan, they came to live with Susan's community in the desert. The men began to build a *laura* nearby, and others moved there to join them.

Concerned by the growing number of hermits and monastics in her area, Susan began to plan to move deeper into the desert. It was decided that a secluded monastery was needed for the women at the edge of this monastic village in order to give them greater solitude from the men. Susan agreed to remain in her cave as long as her privacy was protected. She continued living in her *laura* for another fifteen years, speaking to the monastic community, veiled and from a distance.

Susan was remembered for the strength and wisdom revealed in her teaching as well as for her gift of healing. She held a steadfast and unwavering trust in God's willingness and ability to protect her from the evil one, to deliver her from her own weakness and sin, and to prevail fully in the end. Hers was no feeble Christ.

Susan was known to have lived deep in the desert for twenty-five years before she disappeared from historical records.

SYNCLETICA OF PALESTINE, ANCHORESS

Daughter of an aristocrat in Constantinople, Syncletica was betrothed to another aristocrat when she turned eighteen.[34] As the date of the marriage approached, Syncletica convinced her parents to let her go to "worship at the holy places." She traveled to Jerusalem with a retinue of slaves and eunuchs and three thousand coins. They continued on to the desert of Egypt and visited some of the desert ascetics.

As her retinue was preparing to embark from Jerusalem for Constantinople, Syncletica eluded it by making a pretense of one last visit to the Church of the Resurrection. She walked the highway to Jericho and on to the caves of Copotha. One of the old desert dwellers she had met clothed Syncletica in simple attire and gave her his books, including a two-volume Bible.

Syncletica went off into the desert and found an abandoned cave. She lived alone there for twenty-eight years, known by very few and unseen by anyone. Only Silas of Pharan, a desert ascetic who would later write her Life, knew of her existence, and he reported that Syncletica simply disappeared deeper into the desert.

Syncletica's inner journey focused on cultivating integrity of life: that her outward behavior matched her inner. She fled the frivolous life of her aristocratic circle and dedicated herself fully to seeking God. We know from the details given in her Life that Syncletica is unusual in that gender was not an issue for her: She neither sought to hide her womanhood by choice of clothing or haircut nor focused on it as a challenge or difficulty.

Her feast day is January 5.

TATRE AND KATHARON

An ostracon, pottery with writing on it, found at the monastery of Epiphanius in the Thebes, Egypt, preserves the request of the ascetics Tatre and Katharon to a certain Moses, requesting a portion of a "canon" (this would be a reference to one of the books of what we now call the Bible, which wasn't one book at the time) be sent to them. Contrary to custom, Tatre addresses Moses as "brother" and as "the humblest" rather than the more common "father." Tatre writes the text herself, indicating a certain level of education. The request indicates these women assumed personal responsibility for their spiritual growth. We don't know where Tatre and Katharon lived.[35]

THEODORA

Theodora had been married to a good man but was unfaithful to him. Eventually she was seized with remorse and fled to the desert, disguised as a man. Admitted to a men's monastery under the name of Theodoric, she lived there contently until she was accused of fathering a child. She was expelled from the monastery and lived alone with the baby for seven years. Without revealing her identity, Theodora sought forgiveness and reconciliation with her desert monastic community. She was eventually readmitted to the monastery, where she lived a life of great humility until her death. Only after death was her gender revealed. Her feast day is September 11.

AMMA TRIAISE

Amma Triaise was born in fourth-century Poitou, Gaul, present-day France, to poor parents. Saint Hilary of Poitiers was a close friend and mentor. Amma Triaise made an extended pilgrimage to the main churches of Aquitaine. She settled as a hermit, with few possessions, near Saint Stephens in Rodez. Eventually Florence would become one of her followers. Her feast day is August 16.

VERENE

Verene, an Egyptian, traveled through Europe with her relative, Victor of Thebes. She settled in a cave in the Swiss mountains. Living in complete solitude, she eventually died in 300 CE. Ultimately her remains were transferred to the Church of Saint Stephen in Vienna.

VITALINA OF ARTONA

Vitalina was a solitary of Artona in Auvergne (Gaul) and a friend of Saint Martin of Tours. She died in 390 CE, and her feast is celebrated on February 21.

Chapter Five

DEACONESSES OF THE EARLY CHURCH

The office of deacon has existed since the earliest days of the church. In the first century, women and men serving the people of God in this capacity were called "deacon." Phoebe served the church at Cenchreae as deacon (Rom 16:1). In his First Letter to Timothy, Paul describes the qualifications for anyone aspiring to the ministry, and in the midst of this passage, he states, "Women in this office must likewise…" (1 Tim 3:8–13). Other women are mentioned in Paul's letters as apostles (Prisca, Junia, and Lydia, among other women leaders). Over time and with diverse expressions of Christianity emerging, the gender-specific term *deaconess* began to appear. Initially this was sporadic, and eventually it became the normative reference for women.[1]

Deaconesses were fairly common in the early church. The office evolved over time, mostly due to political and social pressures. Like all offices related to the liturgy, deacons had diverse functions and responsibilities. They ministered to the poor and marginalized, prisoners, widows, and orphans. Some served in significant positions within monastic communities. Some seemed to have served — as they do today in many Christian traditions — along with the presider at Eucharist. Many were actively involved in evangelizing and teaching, training and baptizing female catechumens, and preparing women to receive the sacraments.

Historical records give us the names of many of these deaconesses, sometimes with their geographical locations. Unfortunately, these women are usually just names in records, often in funerary inscriptions. Their history was not recorded or was lost. For example, we know only that Athanasia was a fifth-century deaconess from Delphi, Greece, whose tombstone reads, *"The most devout deaconess Athanasia, established deaconess by his holiness Bishop Pantamianos."* We know of Maria of Moab (present-day Jordan) whose headstone reads, *"Here lies Maria, daughter of Valens, deacon, who lived thirty-eight years and died in the year 538,"*[2] and of Theodora of Gaul, whose tombstone reads, *"Here rests in peace and of good remembrance Theodora the deaconess who lived about forty-eight years and died on 22 July 539,"* who is otherwise unknown. On a tombstone at Aksaray in Cappadocia we read of the deaconess Mary, who *"according to the text of the apostle, raised children, practiced hospitality, washed the feet of the saints and distributed her bread to those in need."*

We know of some deacons from letters that were directed to them by more famous early church leaders. John Chrysostom, while in exile from his see[3] in Constantinople, wrote to "Amproukla deacon,"[4] and Severus of Antioch wrote letters to "Anastasia the deaconess." Bishop and theologian Theodoret of Cyrrhus wrote letters to "Axia, deacon," and to "Casiana, deacon."[5] Placing the exact location of these and many other deacons was most likely problematic, as many church leaders were in exile and the deacons often followed their flocks, ministering to them.

The *Didascalia of the Apostles* and later the *Apostolic Constitutions*[6] mention deacons assisting at baptism, preparing catechumens, instructing women, visiting pagans and believers in their homes, and serving the sick. The Councils of Nicaea (325 CE) and Chalcedon (451 CE), which convened to discuss and clarify significant doctrinal issues around what we now call the Trinity, also clarified some concerns about the ordination of deaconesses. It was decided they were to be at least forty years old, unmarried or widowed, with no dependent children, and impeccable private lives. Deacons were to be scrutinized to verify that they held theological views supportive of the emerging orthodox position. Among the deacons were women who lived in communities of ascetics, the forerunner to Christian monasticism.

The role and position of the deacon within the increasingly institutionalized church was different and distinct from that of the widow and virgin. Widows and virgins were given designated seats in church, just behind the deaconess or deacon. They were acknowledged for their service to the poor and dedication to prayer. Deacons, however, held a more official and liturgical place within the community.

Deaconesses were recognized as ordained in the Eastern Orthodox Church until the eighth or ninth century. However, in the Western Church, deaconesses were not included in the official list of ordained offices by the fourth century. In 441 CE, the Council of Orange forbade the ordination of deaconesses in its region. The Synod of Nîmes declared that the very idea of women claiming to be deacons was so indecent that it would invalidate the whole idea of ordination. In 494 CE, Pope Gelasius wrote a letter to numerous bishops on the need to restrict women ministering at the altar.[7] However, the diaconate continued, even in Gaul. Saint Remigius of Reims (d. 533) mentioned his daughter, the deaconess Helaria, in his will.

Several ancient manuscripts exist, themselves copies of earlier originals, that were used in the ordination of deacons and deaconesses.[8] These show that the rite of ordination was virtually identical, while acknowledging the gender and name of the one being ordained.

Here is one of the prayers recited for the ordination of a deaconess, said as the bishop laid hands on the candidate:

O eternal God, Father of our Lord Jesus Christ, the Creator of man and of woman, who did fill with the Spirit Miriam, Deborah, Anna and Huldah, who did not deem unworthy that your only-begotten Son should be born of a woman, who also in the tent of witness and in the Temple ordained women as keepers of your holy gates: now look upon this your servant who is being ordained as a deaconess, and give her the Holy Spirit, and purify her from any defilement of the flesh and spirit, so that she may worthily accomplish the work entrusted to her and to your glory and the praise of your Christ, with whom to you and to the Holy Spirit be glory and adoration forever. Amen![9]

The following are accounts of some of the church's early deacons. Each was unique in the way she performed her role and ministry.

ANASTASIA THE PATRICIAN

Anastasia was a member of the sixth-century Byzantine aristocracy and the royal court of Emperor Justinian (reigned 527–65 CE) and Empress Theodora. Theodora grew increasingly jealous of Anastasia, who chose to leave Constantinople for Alexandria in Egypt.

Anastasia built a monastery in a neighborhood called Ennaton, about five miles outside of Alexandria. This monastery was known as the Monastery of the Patrician. She lived the discipline of the monastic life, wove cloth to support herself, and served as deaconess.

With the death of Theodora in 548 CE, Justinian began to pursue her. Rather than risk being found, Anastasia went to Scete, deep in the Egyptian desert.[10] There she met with Abba Daniel, who helped her get reestablished away from the probing eyes of the emperor. Anastasia began to wear men's clothing and moved into a *laura* about eighteen miles deeper into the desert. She intended never to leave this cave, and it was arranged for a fellow hermit to bring her jugs of water.

Anastasia lived in solitude for twenty-eight years. As her death approached, she sent word to Abba Daniel to come and bury her. Abba Daniel and his disciple arrived swiftly to share some final words and receive her blessing. She requested and received the Holy Eucharist and a final prayer of blessing from Abba Daniel, turned toward the southeast, stretched out her hands, and said, "O God, into your hands do I commend my soul."[11] Anastasia then made the sign of the cross and died. Her feast day is March 10.

ANNA

In the fifth century, Deacon Anna served alongside her brother, Deacon Dometius, in the church in Rome. As her brother was charged with serving as controller of the monies for the papacy, Anna most likely served in the old Saint Peter's Basilica.

APOLLONIA OF ALEXANDRIA

Deacon Apollonia lived during the third century at a time when Alexandria, a renowned center of learning with a large library, was pagan and was trying to prevent the growth of Christianity. She led many to the faith. When a crowd demanded she affirm her belief in the pagan gods, she was attacked and her teeth were knocked out. She was then put to death by fire. Her feast day is February 9.

BASILINA

We know of Basilina from Cyril of Scythopolis, who had met her. Cappadocian by birth, she was deaconess of the great church of Constantinople, Hagia Sophia. Basilina traveled to Jerusalem with a nephew, a prominent man who was not in communion with Rome. She sought out John the Hesychast in the hope that he would inspire her nephew to rejoin the universal church. As women were not permitted in his presence, John's disciple Theodore escorted the nephew to the *laura*. As a result of John's prophetic ability to read hearts, the nephew was reunited with the church.

Hoping for a personal audience herself, Basilina decided to dress as a man and enter the *laura*. John the Hesychast saw her intent in a prophetic dream. He sent word that he would refuse her visit but would come to her in a dream and converse to her satisfaction. That night Basilina dreamt of John's visit and received the answers she sought.

BRYAINA

Amma Bryaina (sometimes Bryene) was a deaconess who lived with other desert ascetics near Nisibis (Mesopotamia). This was during the time of Emperor Diocletian (d. 311) and his many periods of persecution. She was a disciple of Platonia, who was also a deaconess. Bryaina accepted her orphaned niece, Febronia,[12] to be raised among the ascetics. Bryaina was eventually named leader of the ascetic community and earned a reputation for wisdom. During one of

Emperor Diocletian's persecutions, her niece Febronia was martyred. Bryaina survived.

CELERINA OF CONSTANTINOPLE

In 448 CE, Theodoret of Cyrrhus wrote to Deacon Celerina regarding a delegation of bishops from Syria who were risking travel in winter to present their case in the ongoing christological debates.[13] Deacon Celerina was recognized as politically and theologically influential, and Theodoret urged her to use her sway to further the true faith and protect the peace of the church.

Celerina lived at a time when these complex theological debates were nearly tearing both the church and the empire apart. Theodoret believed and trusted that she could be a calming influence.[14]

CHARITINA OF SAMARIA

The daughter of Epiphanus, Charitina was a deacon connected to a group of ascetics. Most likely in 529 CE during Justinian's (d. 565 CE) suppression of the Samarian revolt, Charitina moved from Samaria to Korykos in Cilicia, Asia Minor (on the southern coast of present-day Turkey). We don't know if she was consecrated a deacon in Samaria or whether this happened in Korykos. A tombstone was dedicated to her. Korykos was home to a considerable number of women ascetics.

DIONYSIA OF MELITENE

Dionysia, a fourth-century woman of noble birth, came from Melitene, a metropolis of Armenia. After many years of marriage, Dionysia was widowed and left with a young son. As her brother, Eudoxius, was the bishop's advisor, Dionysia presented her son, Euthymius (meaning "confidence"), to be raised in the bishop's household. Bishop Otreius then ordained Dionysia as deaconess of his cathedral in Melitene.

DOMNIKA OF CARTHAGE

Domnika was a deaconess who lived during the late fourth century. She was born into a wealthy and prominent Christian Roman family. She rejected marriage and moved to Alexandria in search of meaningful ministry. Domnika befriended four women, nonbelievers who lived in community. These women—Dorothea, Evanthia, Nonna, and Timothea—were seekers and welcomed Domnika into their lives. They eventually converted to Christianity.

They traveled together to Constantinople, where Patriarch Nektarios baptized them and blessed their growing community. They cared for the sick and extended hospitality to travelers. Domnika gained a reputation for her gifts of discernment and prophetic intuition, and for healing the physically and spiritually sick. As the number of pilgrims to the community grew and increasingly interrupted their common life, the women decided to move into the desert. They built a monastery and dedicated the chapel to the prophet Zechariah. At the time of its dedication, Patriarch Nektarios ordained Domnika a deacon. Her feast day is January 8.

ELIZABETH OF NAJRAN

Najran in situated near the border of present-day southwestern Saudi Arabia and Yemen where, in the early sixth century Elizabeth served as deaconess. Her brother, Bishop

Paul, had been martyred in Zafar and his body entombed at the church in Najran where Elizabeth lived.

Due to power plays between the Persian and Byzantine empires, persecution came to her village. The people insisted on hiding her in a house, due to her position as deaconess. When she saw that the church was in flames, she ran out to the church in hopes of saving the relics and other holy objects. She was caught by the regional military authorities, bound, and burned. In a cruel twist of fate, they then tied her feet to a camel, which was driven into the desert (trying to deny believers any more holy relics). Three Christian men slipped out and followed the camel. Finding her dead body, they buried her in an unmarked grave to protect her from further desecration. Her feast day is October 24.

ENEON OF JERUSALEM

Deacon Eneon, daughter of Neoiketes, served at a hospice outside Jerusalem in the village of Siloam. Both churches and monasteries supported hospices for pilgrims, extending hospitality, as well as places to care for the sick and dying. She was buried in Siloam, possibly near the hospice.

EUSEBIA OF CONSTANTINOPLE

Eusebia served as a deacon at the church in Constantinople in the mid-300s CE, living in her own home with a garden "in the front walls of Constantinople." She was originally associated with the "Macedonian sect," a rival claimant to the episcopacy of Constantinople. Sozomen, in his Ecclesiastical History, states that she hid the relics of forty holy martyrs in her own tomb on her property.

EUSEBEIA HOSPITIA

Eusebeia was born in Rome sometime during the fifth century into an aristocratic family of Christians. As she approached the time of an arranged marriage, Eusebeia and two of her slaves began preparations for their flight. She gave most of her personal wealth away to the poor of the city and freed her slaves, making them her equals. They then dressed themselves as men and boarded a boat for Alexandria. From Alexandria they continued to the Greek isle of Kos in the Aegean Sea. They lived in a rented house, resumed wearing women's clothing, and changed their names. Eusebeia became known as Xenia the Merciful.

Meeting an old man at the harbor, Eusebeia convinced him to accept the three women as his disciples. The man was Paul of Mylassa, who was abba of a small monastery in Caria. The women lived in individual cells near the monastery. She fasted for extended periods and spent hours standing in prayer. She was known for being gentle and loving, never impatient or angry.

Eusebeia later built a chapel dedicated to Saint Stephen the First Martyr. Other women eventually joined her community. When Paul became the bishop of Mylassa, he ordained Eusebeia a deaconess. Eusebeia died on January 21 while stretched out in prayer in the monastery chapel. It was said that a dazzling light and sweet incense filled the chapel at the time of her death. She was buried in Sykinon, south of Mylassa. Her feast day is January 24.

GORGONIA OF NAZIANZUS

Gorgonia was the eldest child of Bishop Gregory of Nazianzus the Elder (d. 374 CE) and Deacon Nonna. Her brother was Gregory the Theologian (known as one of the Cappadocian Fathers). She lived a life dedicated to prayer and the study of scripture. After her children were raised, she was ordained a deacon and opened her home to the care of the poor. Her feast day is February 23.

JUSTINA (JUSTA)

The story of Justa is a mixture of history and legend dating from the fourth century.[15] She was born in Antioch, daughter of Aidesios and Cledonia, who were pagans devoted to the Roman Empire's gods and idols. Justa was raised accordingly but soon became a seeker of truth. Convinced of the truth and spiritual power of Jesus's message, Justa was instructed in the Christian faith by the deacon Praylios of Antioch. Soon after her conversion, her parents embraced Christianity as well.

Justa's beauty caught the attention of a highborn and wealthy man, Aglaidas, but she rejected his romantic overtures because he was not a believer. She began monastic observance in her home, cut her hair in the common style of monastics, and observed the seven daily periods of prayer. She began to experience spiritual and physical attacks. Each attack shook her new faith and threatened to diminish her growing inner stillness and quiet. Through her faithfulness to the spiritual journey, Cyprian, the chief sorcerer of the magical arts, was converted to Christianity. He publicly repudiated his past, was soon ordained, and apparently made a bishop to serve the church in the eastern provinces.

As bishop, Cyprian ordained Justa deaconess, renaming her Justina. She became abbess of a monastery of ascetics in Carthage. Justina and Cyprian were eventually arrested for their work of evangelization. Trial and torture took place in Damascus. As they could not be convinced to renounce Christ, they were transferred to Nicomedia to be tried before

Caesar Claudius II (reigned 268–70 CE), and they were beheaded in 268 CE. Their remains were secreted away and buried in Rome by Matrona Rufina, a relative of the emperor. Her feast is October 2.

LAMPADION OF ANNESI

Deacon Lampadion was a member of Macrina the Younger's community, a double monastery of men and women, located in Pontus. She was a close friend of the revered Macrina (d. 379 CE). Lampadian led the community's choir of women. As Macrina lay dying and her brothers were debating whether to bury Macrina in the poor clothing she wore daily or in better clothing, Lampadian interceded and expressed Macrina's wishes.

BLESSED WOMAN MAGNA

In the city of Ancyra of Galatia lived about two thousand women ascetics. Magna[16] was an eminent member of this highly respected group of women. Magna had been married against her will but refused to consummate the marriage. When her husband died, she inherited the full estate and chose to live as an ascetic. Magna was so devoted to serving God that the bishops held her up as an example for all to follow. She was known for her love of voluntary poverty, giving her wealth away to churches, monasteries, and houses for receiving poor strangers, orphans, and widows.

Magna's spirituality was rooted in the imminent return of Christ. She spent much of her time in church awaiting his coming.

MANARIS OF GAZA

Porphyry, bishop of Gaza (d. 420 CE), served at a turbulent time and when Gaza's Christian community was a minority. He was approached by an ill grandmother and her granddaughter, Salaphtha. Each sought baptism from him. Due to the grandmother's poor health, he baptized her immediately and the granddaughter soon thereafter.

Deacon Manaris was summoned by the bishop. The grandmother had died and Salaphtha was orphaned. The bishop charged her with raising and educating Salaphtha in the Christian faith. Deacon Manaris most likely served on the staff of the bishop.

MARIA OF CAPPADOCIA

Maria served as deacon in Archelais, Cappadocia (present-day Turkey), in the sixth century. She was remembered for providing care for children, offering hospitality, assisting at the sacraments, and feeding the poor. Her tombstone is somewhat unique in that the text from 1 Timothy 5:10 is nearly quoted ("she has brought up children, if she has shown hospitality to strangers, if she has washed the saints' feet, if she has assisted those in distress, and if she has devoted herself to every good work").[17]

MARTHANA

Marthana lived in the fourth century and was a dear friend, colleague, and equal of Egeria, whose wrote a travelogue of her pilgrimage from Spain to the holy sites in Egypt and Palestine.[18] They originally met in Jerusalem. Marthana was deaconess at the shrine to Saint Thecla near Seleucia, present-day Turkey. She was also the spiritual leader of a double monastery of both men and women. Each lived in an individual cell as a solitary, observing strict asceticism.

MATRONA OF COSILA

The fourth-century deacon Matrona served at a shrine dedicated to John the Baptist in Cosila, near Chalcedon in present-day Turkey. She was involved in a political tug-of-war with the emperor Valens (d. 378) and subsequently with the emperor Theodosius (d. 379) over the relics she protected. She eventually lost the political battle, and the relics were moved to Constantinople. Matrona remained in Cosila and served as leader of a group of ascetics.

NONNA OF NAZIANZUS

Deacon Nonna was the wife of Bishop Gregory of Nazianzus the Elder and mother of Gorgonia and Gregory the Theologian.[19] It was Nonna who led her husband to become a Christian and who corrected some of his misunderstandings of the Christian faith. She was a woman of deep prayer who extended hospitality to those in need. She died in church while in prayer. Her feast day is August 5.

OLYMPIAS

Born in 365 CE in the region of Constantinople, Turkey, to Seleucus, an imperial officer and prominent member of court circles, Olympias[20] was orphaned young. She was quite wealthy, with extensive lands in Thrace, Galatia, Cappadocia,

Bithynia, and in Constantinople. Olympias was well educated, as was expected of members of the Imperial court.

Olympias was married briefly to Nebridius, prefect of Constantinople, but they apparently never consummated this marriage. After the death of her husband, Olympias was accused before her relative, Emperor Theodosius, "of dispensing her goods in a disorderly fashion."[21] Theodosius tried to force her to marry one of his relatives, Elpidius. Olympias gave a wonderfully independent response to Emperor Theodosius:

> If my King, the Lord Jesus Christ, wanted me to be joined with a man, he would not have taken away my first husband immediately. Since he knew that I was unsuited for the conjugal life and was not able to please a man, he freed him, Nebridius, from the bond and delivered me of this very burdensome yoke and servitude to a husband, having placed upon my mind the happy yoke of continence.[22]

When Theodosius failed to force Olympias into a new marriage, he placed her possessions under the protection of the prefect Clementinus until she turned thirty. This prefect denied her access to the church and the opportunity to meet with notable bishops. Theodosius hoped to coerce Olympias into a new marriage, but she responded to the emperor and the prefect,

> You have shown toward my humble person, O sovereign master, a goodness befitting a king and suited to a bishop, when you commanded my very heavy burden to be put under careful guard, for the administration of it caused me anxiety. But you will do even better if you order that it be distributed to the poor and to the churches, for I prayed much

to avoid the vainglory arising from the apportion-
ment, lest I neglect true riches for those pertaining
to material things.[23]

In 391 CE, Theodosius restored Olympias's right to control her personal wealth, allegedly because of her reputation
for ascetic discipline. Olympias began to distribute her wealth
to the poor, to establish monastic communities, and endow
churches. Her biographer tells us,

> For no place, no country, no desert, no island, no
> distant setting, remained without a share in the
> benevolence of this famous woman; rather, she
> furnished the churches with liturgical offerings
> and helped the monasteries and convents, the beg-
> gars, the prisoners, and those in exile; quite simply,
> she distributed her alms over the entire inhabited
> world. And the blessed Olympias herself burst the
> supreme limit in her almsgiving and her humility,
> so that nothing can be found greater than what she
> did.[24]

After Olympias gave away a sizable portion of her wealth
in gold, silver, and real estate, Bishop Nectarius ordained her
deacon of the Cathedral of Hagia Sophia (Holy Wisdom) in
Constantinople.[25] She still owned all the property—houses
and shops—at the south edge of the cathedral, where she
built a monastery for herself.

Fifty of her chambermaids joined her in the monastic
life. Her sisters, Martyria and Palladia, as well as another relative, Elisanthia, also joined her. Eventually, her niece Olym-
pia and many other women of senatorial families joined, and
this monastery eventually grew to include 250 members. While
her monastery was being constructed, Elisanthia, Martyria, and
Palladia were also made deacons of the cathedral.

Olympias was as renowned for her asceticism as for her generosity and disposal of her goods. She and her community were known for their faithfulness to prayer, their inner peace, and their firmness of conviction. As was common among ascetics, Olympias slept little, bathed rarely, abstained from eating meat, and wore only the simplest clothing of inferior quality. Despite treating her body harshly, Olympias was known for her gentleness of spirit.

Olympias's biographer describes her as

> full of every reverence, bowing before the saints, venerating the bishops, honoring the presbyters, respecting the priests, welcoming the ascetics, being anxious for the virgins, supplying the widow, raising the orphans, shielding the elderly, looking after the weak, having compassion on sinners, guiding the lost, having pity on all, pity without stinting anything on the poor. Engaging in much catechizing of unbelieving women and making provision for all the necessary things of life, she left a reputation for goodness throughout her whole life, which is ever to be remembered. Having called from slavery to freedom her myriad household servants, she proclaimed them to be of the same honor as her own nobility.[26]

Olympias's monastic life centered upon learning, prayer, service to the poor, and ascetic practices. John Chrysostom and other theologians found her an able colleague with whom they could debate and explore theological issues. Many sought her counsel, and she influenced the affairs of the church.

Chrysostom is primarily remembered as a brilliant preacher in the churches of his native Antioch and as a powerful bishop of Constantinople, a stern proponent of the ascetic life, critic of luxury and corruption, and a prolific writer.

Olympias remained his friend and supporter during his exile when he suffered from loneliness and depression. Chrysostom felt deeply the separation from his close friends, including Olympias. When ousted from Constantinople for his unpopular attempts at moral reform in 404 CE, Chrysostom found Olympias his chief defender. Chrysostom remained in exile, traveling around eastern Turkey until his death in 407. Olympias continued to support him and his followers in exile.

In Chrysostom's letters to Olympias, we learn that his exile drove her to despair and bouts of depression. In his attempts to inspire her with hope, Chrysostom spoke of his only suffering being Olympias's unhappiness expressed in the too few letters he received from her. He writes,

> This is one way in which you can show your affection for me....I want you to show the same cheerfulness as I saw in you when we were together. For you are well aware how much you will restore me if you succeed in this and can show it openly in your letters to me.[27]

Olympias was friend and supporter of some notable people who significantly shaped the development of Christianity: Gregory of Nyssa, Basil the Great, and Macrina.[28] Her teacher, Theodosia, was a friend and correspondent of Basil and cousin of Gregory of Nazianzus.[29] Gregory of Nazianzus, while bishop of Constantinople, dedicated a poem to her. Gregory of Nyssa dedicated part of his commentary on the Song of Songs to her. Her biographer, writing soon after her death in 410 describes Olympias in the following words:

> A partner of the divine Word, a consort of every true humility, a companion and servant of the holy, catholic and apostolic Church of God.[30]

And,

> She had a life without vanity, an appearance without pretense, character without affectation, a face without adornment; she kept watch without sleeping, she had an immaterial body, a mind without vainglory, intelligence without conceit, an untroubled heart, an artless spirit, charity without limits, unbounded generosity, contemptible clothing, immeasurable self-control, rectitude of thought, undying hope in God, ineffable almsgiving; she was the ornament of all the humble.[31]

And,

> ...Full of simplicity and humility,
> Untiring in her works of mercy,
> Radiating love, modest, calm,
> And of infinite generosity.[32]

Her feast day is July 25.

PLATONIDA OF SYRIA

Platonida served as a deacon of the Mesopotamian Church but eventually moved into the Nisibis desert to live as a desert ascetic. Other women joined her. The rule she wrote was known for its strictness, eating once daily and, when not in prayer, working at various labors to support the community. The community was known for its gracious hospitality. She died in 308 CE and her feast day is April 6.

PENTADIA OF CONSTANTINOPLE

Pentadia was ordained a deacon sometime after the death of her exiled husband while continuing as head of her household. She was a friend of John Chrysostom and during his forced exile (404–7 CE), he wrote several letters to her and in one asked, "Why haven't I heard from you?" Palladius places Deacon Pentadia along with Deacons Procla[33] and Olympias in the Cathedral when Chrysostom was forced into exile.

POPLIA OF ANTIOCH

Poplia (or Publia) lived in fourth-century Antioch. Married with children, she earned a reputation for the strength of her faith and her spiritual discipline. Sometime after the death of her husband, Poplia was ordained a deacon. Her home became a monastery, where she served as choir director. There were several deacons in the community.

Poplia, in her later years, confronted the Emperor Julian the Apostate (d. 363 CE) by arranging for her community to chant Psalm 135 as his retinue passed by. He heard, "The gods of the nations are idols of silver and gold, fashioned by human hands" (v. 15) and again "The gods of the nations are idols of silver and gold, fashioned by human hands" (v. 15). The emperor ordered them to cease, and instead they chanted, "May God rise and his enemies scattered, and those hostile to him flee at his approach. You disperse them like smoke; you melt them like wax near fire. The wicked perish at the presence of God" (Ps 68:1–2). The emperor, in his rage, ordered her struck on both sides of her face, bloodying her.[34] The community sang even more insistently until the frustrated Julian left. Her feast day is October 9.

POSIDONIA

Posidonia served as deacon in the fourth to fifth centuries in Philippi, Macedonia. Her tombstone survived until sometime after 1889 CE and bore an unusual inscription: "Illustrious graves of Posidonia, deacon, and Pancharia, the last canoness." Rarely used in the early church, a canoness lived in an informal ascetic community without formal vows or ordination and ministered to the local community; sometimes serving as lector as well.[35] Why were these two women interred together? Scholars wonder: Did Deacon Posidonia serve in some kind of pastoral role to Pancharia's community? Were they friends?

Posidonia is commemorated in a mosaic in the baptistery of Saint Lydia, located near the ancient archeological site of Philippi in present-day Greece.

ROMANA OF ANTIOCH

Romana, a highborn woman, was the senior deaconess serving with the bishop of Antioch. When the actress Pelagia[36] converted, Bishop Nonnus sent for Romana, who instructed Pelagia in the faith and was present for her baptism. Pelagia lived with Romana for a while, receiving further support and instruction in the faith during the early days of her new life. Once Pelagia disappeared into the desert, Romana moved to Jerusalem and constructed a cell for herself on the Mount of Olives.

SABINIANA OF ANTIOCH

Sabiniana lived as a solitary in Antioch, an active center of the Christian movement. She was the aunt of John

Chrysostom, patriarch of Constantinople, who referred to her as "my lady Sabiniana, the deaconess." She joined Chrysostom in exile in Scythia. Palladius, who had met her while visiting Antioch, wrote in his *Lausiac History* that she was "a most venerable woman, on intimate terms with God."

SEVERA OF JERUSALEM

Severa was a deaconess and member of the monastic community in Jerusalem that had been founded and guided by Melania the Elder. At some point during her monastic observance, Severa and several companions decided to become wandering ascetics. Evagrius Ponticus wrote a letter to Melania expressing his concerns both for their safety and for the wisdom of monastic wandering—a form of asceticism in the East.

SOFIA, "THE SECOND PHOEBE"

Sofia (d. 562) served as deacon in one of the churches in Jerusalem. Her work as a deacon was documented by Egeria, a Christian pilgrim who visited Jerusalem in the early 400s and carefully recorded her encounters with Christian leaders such as Sofia. Her headstone, found on the Mount of Olives in 1903 and now in the museum of Saint Anne's Church in Jerusalem, was thus inscribed: "the Second Phoebe,"[37] a rare honor.

SUSANNA

Susanna was born in Palestine in the latter part of the third century. Her father, Artemios, was a rich pagan priest.

Her mother, Martha, brought her up in the Jewish faith. When her parents died, Susanna was placed under guardianship until she married.

After many conversations with her neighbor, Silvanos, Susanna decided to become a Christian and was baptized. She gained control of her wealth, gave much to the poor, and set all her slaves free. She cropped her hair short, donned men's clothing, took the name John, and presented herself at a men's monastery in Jerusalem. The monks assumed she was a eunuch, and Susanna was accepted.

Susanna matured in her monastic observance and eventually became superior of the monastery. Twenty years into her faithful service, a visiting nun fell in love with Susanna and tried to win her affections. When this failed, the nun accused Susanna of seducing her. The local bishop, Kleopas, was called in along with two deaconesses from Eleutheropolis in southern Judea. Susanna revealed her gender to the deaconesses and her name was cleared. The bishop was so impressed with Susanna that he brought her back with him to his cathedral. There he ordained Susanna deaconess and appointed her abbess of a small monastery. She served as spiritual elder for many years, served the poor, extended hospitality, and prayed for the healing of many.

Eventually Susanna was arrested for refusing to offer sacrifices to the gods. She died in prison during the reign of Julian the Apostate (d. 363 CE). Her feast is September 19.

THEODULA OF TABENNISI

Deacon Theodula lived in the desert of Egypt. She led a small community of ascetics and was renowned for the power of her prayer and for a ministry of healing. The community was well educated and expected anyone who joined them to make learning part of their ascetical practice.

Through some powerful dreams, Theodula "saw" the impending death of some of the ascetics in her community and then, in 410 CE, she saw her own impending death. Thus, Theodula called together her fellow ascetics, announced she would die soon, and asked them to name her successor. Theogneia was chosen. Theodula prayed over her successor, the community entered their oratory, and Theodula ordered them to stay away until the following morning. The next day, they found her dead.

It was customary, in writing the lives of saints, to attribute to them foreknowledge of their own death, a sign of the saints' "power over death."

THEOPHILA OF ASĒRMOS

Asērmos was a village in Crimea and located on the Black Sea where Theophila served as deacon. She lived during the reign of Constantine (d. 337 CE). As part of her ministry, she brought an ascetic, Rufina, to the bishop, Parthenius of Lampsacus, to pray for her healing. The two prayed for Rufina's healing for three days, sprinkling holy water on her. Rufina was healed and able to return to her village.

Theophila filled a role common to deacons: to accompany the sick on pilgrimage to places and persons with healing power.

THEOSEBIA

Theosebia, the wife[38] of Gregory of Nyssa, was ordained a deacon at the same time as her husband was ordained a bishop in 371 CE. She was influential in church matters and revered for her wisdom. She arranged for the care of the sick and orphans, distributed food to the hungry, and prepared women for baptism. She died in 385 CE. Her feast day is January 10.

TIMOTHEA

Timothea served as a deacon in Korykos, Celicia, and was most likely a leader of a group of women ascetics. She was buried in a tomb, created just for herself, which indicates that she was held in highest esteem.

VETIANA

Vetiana was of noble birth, extremely wealthy, and quite beautiful. The daughter of Senator Araxios, she was married to Aguilo, commander of the infantry and of equal social rank. When Araxios died in 366 CE, Vetiana joined Macrina[39] in the monastic life in Cappadocia while also maintaining a residence in Constantinople. She was present at Macrina's death and, along with Lampadion,[40] made the burial arrangements.

Chapter Six

MENTORS OF THE MONASTIC WAY

Communities and Their Leaders

I do not view monasticism as a retreat from the world
but as an entry into its beating heart.

—Elise Boulding, in A *Monastic Year*[1]

The first monastic communities evolved around a single
charismatic personality, oftentimes a desert ascetic. Others
were complex webs of relationships among many gifted
women. Many monasteries included hermits. Others were
in close contact with desert ascetics. In recognition of the
communal nature of monasticism, I have grouped the
following stories by geographic location.

NORTH AFRICA

Egypt

Both desert ascetics and monasticism were long associated with the regions of Egypt. While some ascetics lived

alone most of their adult life, others grouped near one another in caves. Monastic communities in Egypt were a blend of desert ascetics who lived in caves nearby with occasional contact with their monasteries or lived in seclusion within the monastic complex, and those who lived in community, gathering together for prayer and working alongside one another. A smaller number of ascetics entered deep into the desert with minimal contact with the human community.

While little detail survives regarding the specifics of women in the emerging monastic movement, archeologists claim that many women's monastic communities were found along the Nile River. Many of these cells and groupings of cells were crafted from abandoned and ancient palaces or tombs. Women's and men's communities were situated near each other and swapped services.

Anthony the Great (251–356 CE) left his village, named Tkmene, and traveled into the Egyptian desert in search of a deeper relationship with the Divine. His "Outer Mountain," located west of the Nile River and his "Inner Mountain," located on the eastern side of the Nile River, both near Alexandria, drew attention to this "desert." His fame grew, attracting others to seek a solitary life in the desert.

He was credited with the founding of eremitic monasticism, sometimes referred to as desert monasticism. When individuals wanted to learn "the way of the desert," they sought out an elder and lived in a cave nearby. The number of followers often grew and as they were grouped around one elder, this became known as eremitic monasticism. The emphasis was this one-on-one relationship between this elder and each of his followers. The Egyptian desert was dotted with many ascetics, but Anthony became the most famous of these early leaders due to a biography written by Bishop Athanasius (d. 373 CE) of Alexandria.

Pachomian Foundations

Pachomius (292–348 CE) is credited with the founding of Christian cenobitic monasticism, which is expressed in communal living with a chosen leader and usually a rule of life.[2] After years of service to the poor of his village, he became a disciple of Abba Palamon in 316 CE. After seven years he had traveled through a large acacia forest, continuing on for about ten miles until he came to a deserted village known as Tabennesi on the shore of the Nile. Over time Pachomius attracted followers and a monastic village emerged.

While Anthony and Pachomius are credited with establishing forms of Christian monasticism, they each placed a sister in a community of ascetic women in order to go off and live an ascetic life. It was their biographies (called *Lives*) and Pachomius's *Rule* that grew in popularity around the Roman Empire that led to crediting them with establishing Christian monasticism.

Amma Mary

Mary was the sister of Pachomius. Fifteen years after her brother departed from their village, she had heard he had settled in this abandoned village of Tabennesi. Arriving, she discovered that a monastic complex of men had developed, all followers of her brother. Inquiring of her brother at the gate, which was staffed by one of the monks, she was given Pachomius's response:

> I see you have learned I am alive. Do not be distressed, however, because you have not seen me. But if you wish to share in this holy life so that you may find mercy before God, examine yourself on every point. The brothers will build a place for you to retire to. And doubtless, for your sake the Lord will call others to you, and they will be saved because of you. We have no other hope in this world but to do

good before we depart from our body and are led to the place where we shall be judged and rewarded according to our works.[3]

Women heard of what Mary had done and joined her. A monastery, with its own separate chapel, was built nearby for Mary and her increasing number of followers. Pachomius sent her a copy of his *Rule* that he and his disciples followed. The women supported themselves with manual labor—they were responsible for the production of textiles and garments for both the women and men of the community—while maintaining times for prayer and fasting. Contact with the monks was limited, and when family members wanted to visit one another, they were accompanied by a member of their monastery. When one of the nuns died, the community of women prepared the deceased for burial, chanting the psalms while wrapping her body in a shroud. The monks came and carried her bier to the mountain for burial, the nuns following and chanting psalms. These precautions were created as the nuns and monks were trying to protect their reputation in the midst of a hostile empire. History does not record when Amma Mary died.

Pachomius established a second community of women nearby in Tsmine, but history fails to record which women served as leader or anything else about the monastery's history.

The White Monastery

In the mid-fourth century, two ascetics, Abba Pgol and Abba Pschai, lived in the desert near Smin, located along the Nile River just south of Alexandria. Around 385 CE these men transformed their cells into two monastic communities: Abba Pgol established the White Monastery in the Theban desert near the ruined village of Atripe, and Abba Pschai established the Red Monastery on the mountain Psou. The names referred to the color of their complexes.

The White Monastery consisted of a men's monastery and a women's monastery. Abba Pgol's nephew, Shenoute (348–464 CE), became leader about 385 CE. The community grew to around 2,200 men and 1,800 women. The *Rule* Pgol created was far more austere than Pachomius's *Rule*, which was followed by many neighboring monasteries of women and men. Pgol's *Rule*, however harsh, treated women as fully equal to men. All goods and food were shared equally between the men's and women's communities. As part of their commitment ceremony, they signed a document renouncing all possessions and any future inheritances would come directly to the community, not the individual.

When Shenoute became leader, he sought to exercise control over the women's community, which Abba Pgol had not, and this caused great trouble. The tone of his few surviving letters[4] to the women's community sound severe. Shenoute pressed for long and harsh fasts, which some nuns resisted on behalf of frailer members. He complained about the shape and quality of the garments the nuns crafted for the monks while admitting he didn't permit the nuns to come near the monks in order to take proper measurements. Shenoute was a great proponent of corporal punishment for infractions of his *Rule* (for everyone), and the punishment was meted out by the monks upon the nuns (during the rare times that they were actually in the same space) in the gatehouse, where new members lived. Scholars suggest this served two purposes: to mete out the punishment in front of new members to impress upon them the seriousness of an infraction of one of his rules, and as a subtle threat of being demoted in rank.

Some women did go off into the desert to live a life of solitude as extended members of the White Monastery. And like Shenoute, they returned four times a year for community meetings.

The women had maintained an active relationship with Pachomius's Red Monastery, primarily for spiritual teaching, welcoming the monks into their home. But the women had minimal contact with the monks of the White Monastery, only to receive "the materials for the Eucharist," until Shenoute was elected. He made it his business to interfere with the internal life of the nuns. Yet he did clearly see the nuns as fully equal to his monks. Apparently he treated them all the same.

Amma Tachom

Amma Tachom was one of the leaders of the women's community with a reputation for strong and unwavering leadership. For reasons unknown to us, Abba Shenoute tried to appoint a priest of his community as her community's leader against her will. Amma Tachom refused to meet with this cleric and a battle over authority and the right to self-determination ensued. She had a sense of what was best for her community. She recognized the damaging effect of Shenoute's autocratic attempts at exercising authority within her community. His response was to mock her. She stood firm.

It is possible that this is a shadow of the cultural shift in which women who had been presiding at their own community's prayers were forcibly ousted and replaced by male clerics.

Amma Aphthonia

All we know of Amma Aphthonia is from a letter sent to her by Besa, Shenoute's successor, chastising her for her acceptance of a gift from her parents. Apparently she did not turn the gift over to leadership "fast enough."

Amma Sansno

We know of Amma Sansno because Shenoute had chastised her for teaching others and admitting to doing so. Shenoute seemed to think that only he and he alone could be called "Teacher," while contradicting himself by admitting that the leader of the women's community was also "Teacher."

Other women monastics were identified in his letters as Amma Taese, Amma Tsaneno, Amma Dschenbiktor, Amma Apolle, Amma Tsophia and Amma Tapolle (sisters), Amma Maria, and Amma Theodora.[5] But other than their names we know nothing.

Antinoë

Antinoë, located along the Nile River in upper Egypt in the region of the Thebaid, was home to at least twelve monastic communities of women.

Blessed Mother Talida

For eighty years, Mother Talida (sometimes translated as Talis) resided in a monastic community with sixty other women. This community was known as a happy, harmonious, affectionate, and love-filled home. It was rare for anyone to leave. The women were deeply devoted to Talida, who was renowned for her teaching, her ascetic excellence, and the quality of spiritual formation of her sisters. Grounded in the freedom and confidence of her faith, Talida exercised a quiet boldness in dealing with others.

Unlike the restrictions placed upon women ascetics in the monasteries of Pachomius or Shenoute, Mother Talida was comfortable with receiving men as guests and her reputation was never compromised.

The Virgin Taor

Taor was a disciple of Mother Talida and lived in the same monastery for thirty years. Renowned for her beauty and graceful manners, Taor never went out in public and preferred rags to new clothing. Her dedication to solitude in her urban desert was so intense that she refused to go to town with her community on the first day of the week to partake in the Offering (Mass).

The Unknown Ascetic

This unknown ascetic lived a life of such solitude that Palladius[6] stated that he had never seen her face. After living thus for sixty years, the Holy Spirit informed her that she would soon die and that she should go at dawn to the chapel dedicated to the martyr Colluthus,[7] who was the patron saint of Antinoë, to prepare for her passing from this life into the next: "This day you will make the journey to the Master and see all the saints. Come, then, and eat with us in the chapel."[8] She took a basket of bread, olives, and chopped vegetables. She prayed in the chapel all day, and when she was alone, she ate the food and returned home at sunset. She gave her mother writings she had composed on Clement of Alexandria's writings[9] on the prophet Amos. She died that night.

Evidence of monastic communities and ascetic cells in the Theban desert region of Egypt has been of great interest to archeologists. Ascetics and monastic communities made use of the ruins of Pharaonic temples, and there are ongoing excavations and study of underground monasteries. Evidence left behind demonstrates that Christian ascetics remained active in the area well into the eighth century, even in the midst of the rise of Islam. Archeologists also maintain that it was the desert ascetics who were responsible for most of the education—in both Coptic and Greek—in the area. The influence of literary sources was traced back to them. Pieces of correspondence unearthed refer to "Amma Sophia," "Amma Maria," "Amma Theophile," and "Amma Mariam," discussing children left in their care (or in the care of neighboring monks who wanted to hand the children off to the women), handling real estate matters, or transactions regarding goods bought and sold. All referred to ordinary business, which tells scholars that the presence of self-supporting women ascetics in the area was considered normal.

Hippo

Augustine of Hippo[10] was born in Thagaste (present-day Algeria) to a Romanized Berber family and completed his education in Carthage (present-day Tunisia). His dramatic conversion story and subsequent spiritual journey were well documented through his many writings. As a renowned teacher and preacher, and later as bishop, Augustine was in contact with many women's communities in Africa. Unfortunately, not many names survived history and certainly nothing of their personal lives.

Amma Felicitas

Augustine had a sister who was leader of a woman's community near Hippo. No surviving source named her. Upon her death, a nun named Felicitas assumed leadership. After a few years, internal troubles erupted and Augustine found it necessary to send a letter to Amma Felicitas encouraging her in the midst of these challenges. He then wrote a letter to the community, reminding them that their internal strife must come to an end and to support Amma Felicitas.[11] Her voice is lost to history. The letter goes on to describe his vision of healthy religious community, and this became the basis of what is now known as the Rule of Augustine.[12]

ASIA MINOR

Asia Minor was a crossroad for the trade route between the Roman Empire and the Far East. Roads crisscrossed this region to support trade and the activities of the Roman military.

Cappadocia, an important region of Asia Minor, was located in present-day Turkey. The region is mountainous yet is also blessed with rivers and rich farmland. The nobility owned profitable estates and summer homes in Cappadocia.

CAPPADOCIA

Macrina the Younger

One of the earliest monastic communities was founded and developed by an aristocratic family of Christians. It began on their estates at Annisa near the Black Sea. Macrina the Younger was the original inspiration and genius behind this development.

Macrina's family was already renowned for its financial support of fellow persecuted Christians and its faithful leadership during the difficult time of Diocletian's persecution. Macrina's grandmother, Macrina the Elder, worked closely with the bishop in Pontus, Gregory Thaumaturgus (the Wonder Worker). Macrina's parents were Emmelia, who managed the family estates and oversaw Macrina's education, and Basil, bishop and teacher of rhetoric. Emmelia and Basil continued the family dedication to extending hospitality and caring for the poor and sick, as well as to an intense life of prayer.

Born in 327 CE, Macrina was the eldest of many children. When her fiancé died, she resolved to live a life of asceticism. After her father died in 340, she assisted her mother in running the household and estates. Macrina became a pillar of strength for the family.

Macrina's continued dedication to asceticism would eventually encompass the full household. She began to simplify the family's lifestyle, giving away many of the trappings of their social class. She lived with her household as one in Christ, servants and slaves treated as equals. She wore the same clothing, slept in a similar type of bed, made do with the minimum of necessities of life, and shared a table for meals. Emmelia and Macrina took on the pastoral care of the household.

Macrina pursued her brothers, especially Basil and Gregory of Nyssa, until they accepted baptism.[13] When Basil returned from his studies in Athens with a head swelled with pride, she cut him down to size. They all acknowledged her as the primary influence in their theological education, and each finally embraced ascetic and monastic observance. Basil would codify their way of life into a series of conferences on the monastic life known as the *Short* and *Long Rules*. Basil, later known as the Great, is credited as the founder of Eastern Monasticism, though Macrina actually started the movement.

The family estate at Annisa grew into the center of their monastic observance that became known as the "School of Virtue." The women gathered around Macrina and Emmelia and lived in a compound on one side of the river Iris; the men, gathered around her brother, Peter of Sebaste, lived in a compound on the other. Scholars are unable to determine the exact layout of these compounds, and the ratio of solitary ascetics to those living communally is unknown.

The communities cultivated gardens for quiet and meditation. Gregory wrote of a particularly favored garden spot with an arbor of climbing vines.

They worshiped together — at least some of the time — in a shared church. The communities prayed the psalms throughout the day: on rising in the morning, when beginning their work and when resting from it, and before and after meals. The community prayed the Evening Office of Thanksgiving as the lamps were lit.

Macrina insisted that her community support itself through manual labor and not live off the work of others. She baked the community bread as well as the bread for Eucharist.

Her personal wealth was administered by another and was used to feed the poor.

Macrina's biographer, speaking of her monastic observance, tells us,

> Just as souls, when released from bodies by death, are freed at the same time from the cares of this life, so was their life similarly liberated. It was lived apart from all worldly trivialities and was brought into harmony with the life of the angels.[14]

And,

> For neither anger nor envy nor hatred nor pride nor anything else of that kind was ever seen in them; the desire for earthly vanities, honor, glory, pride and everything of that kind had been banished. Their delight was in self-control; their glory was to be unknown; their wealth was to possess nothing, having shaken off all material superfluity from their bodies as though it were dust. Their work...consisted only of attention to the things of God, prayer without ceasing, and the uninterrupted chanting of the Psalms, which was extended equally in time through night and day, so that for the virgins it was both work and rest from work.[15]

The most gifted and brilliant of her brothers, Naucratios, with his servant Chrysaphios, left public life and lived a quiet life as an ascetic in a simple shelter in the dense woods on a cliff above Iris River. They both accepted responsibility for caring for a group of poor and ill peasants nearby. Emmelia served as their pastoral and spiritual guide. Naucratios died in a hunting accident while trying to secure provisions for the poor. The family and community were deeply grieved.

According to Gregory,

> They say that the testing of gold takes place in dif-
> ferent furnaces, so that if any impurity escapes the
> first smelting, it is separated in the second, and once
> more in the final smelting, when the substance is
> purged of every impurity that is mixed with it. The
> most accurate proof that gold has been properly
> tested is that it throws up no further impurity after
> it has been through every melting pot. What hap-
> pened to Macrina was of similar character. The lofty
> nature of her thought was tried from every direction
> by successive blows of fortune, but she displayed
> purity and steadfastness of soul….She remained
> firm, like an athlete who could not be defeated, and
> never flinched as the blows of fortune.[16]

Gregory became a bishop and soon developed much
of our early theology of the Holy Spirit and mysticism. With
Basil, he was a major leader in the movement in support of
the Council of Nicaea, which developed the Nicene Creed
to combat the Arian heresy. He faced intermittent persecution from supporters of Arius and the Arian movement. The
Roman emperor supported the Arians, and this placed Gregory in an uncomfortable opposition. Macrina exhorted him,
with dry humor, to stand firm, just as their grandparents did
before them:

> Will you not put an end to your failure to recognise
> the good things which come from God?…
>   Churches send you forth and call upon you as
> ally and reformer, and you do not see the grace in this?
> Do you not even realise the true cause of such great
> blessings, that our parents' prayers are lifting you on
> high, for you have little or no native capacity for this?[17]

Macrina was renowned for giving clear-headed counsel during difficult times of political and theological upheaval in the church. Recognized for being intellectually capable (some scholars speak of her as a genius), she was often referred to as "the Teacher." She ably handled cruel food shortages in her region. Macrina inspired deep affection in others. Many sought her out for spiritual counsel.

Gregory records some of Macrina's teachings for us in a document entitled *On the Soul and the Resurrection*.[18] In classic philosophical fashion, Macrina ponders the nature of the human soul and what happens after death. Her teachings reflect both the depth of her understanding and her use of common human experience to express her thought.

As she approached death, Macrina's bed was turned toward the East in anticipation of the resurrection. She stopped speaking with others, and only spoke to God in prayer. Her brother Gregory was with her, and he saw Macrina stretch out her hands to her Beloved in supplication and say in a gentle, barely audible undertone,

Macrina's Prayer

It is you, O Lord, who have freed us from the fear of death. You have made our life here the beginning of our true life. You grant our bodies to rest in sleep for a season and you rouse our bodies *again at the last trumpet.*

You have given in trust to the earth our earthly bodies, which you have formed with your own hands, and you have restored what you have given, by transforming our mortality and ugliness by our immortality and your grace.

You have delivered us from the curse of the law and from sin, by being made both on our behalf. You have *broken the dragon's head*—that dragon who seized man by the throat and dragged him through the yawning gulf of disobedience. You have opened for us the way of the resurrection, after breaking the gates of hell, and have destroyed him that had the power of death.

You have given as a token to those who fear you the image of the holy cross, to destroy the adversary and to bring stability to our lives.

Eternal God, for whom I was snatched from my mother's womb, whom my soul loved with all its strength, to whom I consecrated my flesh from my youth until now, entrust to me an angel of light, who will lead me by the hand to the place of refreshment, where the "water of repose" is, in the bosom of the holy patriarchs.

May you, who cut through the fire of the flaming sword and assigned to paradise him who was crucified with you and entrusted to your pity, remember me too in your kingdom, because I too have been crucified with you; from fear of you I have nailed down my flesh and have been in fear of your judgements.

May the terrible gulf not separate me from those whom you have chosen, nor may the malignant Enemy set himself across my path, nor may my sin be discovered in your sight, if having error through the weakness of our human nature, I have committed any sin in word or in deed.

May you who have power on earth to forgive sins, forgive me, that I may draw breath and that I be found in your presence, "having shed my body and without spot or wrinkle" in the form of my soul, and that my soul may be innocent and spotless and may be received into your hands *like incense in your presence*.[19]

Scholars believe that Macrina had spoken many portions of this prayer during her lifetime, and that Gregory wove these prayers and her teachings together in Macrina's honor.

As evening drew near and the lamps were lit, members of Macrina's community began the Evening Office of Thanksgiving in her presence. As the prayers concluded, Macrina sighed deeply and died.

A solemn procession from the women's monastery to the church included the local population and clergy and lasted all day. Candles were lit and psalms chanted while they were in procession. Bishop Araxios presided at her funeral. Macrina was buried in the Church of the Holy Martyrs, next to her parents. Her feast day is July 19.

CONSTANTINOPLE

Elisabeth the Wonderworker

Elisabeth was born to aging parents, Euphemia and Eunomianos. While scholars do not know the exact date of her birth or her death, we do know that she was a contemporary of Gennadios I, patriarch of Constantinople from 458 to 471 CE; of Leo I, Byzantine emperor from 457 to 474 CE; and of Daniel the Stylite, who arrived in Constantinople around 451 CE. Her family owned an estate in Abydenoi, near Herakleia in Thrace, and was known for their hospitality to the poor, giving liberally to those in need. Her parents invested heavily in Elisabeth's education, which included scripture.

Elisabeth's mother died when she was twelve; her father died when she was fifteen. Although she inherited her family's wealth, she decided to join her aunt's monastic community. She gave her silver and gold to the poor, distributed her other considerable property, and set her slaves free.

Elisabeth joined her aunt in Constantinople, whose monastery was located on "Little Hill." Saint George was its patron saint. She began her monastic observance, fasting, bathing rarely, embracing poverty, and going without shoes (significant for one of her social class). Elisabeth grew in humility and in freedom from passions. When her aunt died, she was appointed abbess.

Elisabeth quickly became known for her prophetic and healing powers. She was especially effective in praying for women who suffered from an excessive flow of blood and for the blind. This ministry continued for many years.

Elisabeth made a final visit to her familial estates to see family and pray at holy sites. She had been made aware of her impending death through a dream. Upon returning to her monastic community, Elisabeth died of an intense fever on the twenty-fourth of April. She was buried in the Cathedral of Saint George, and her body remained incorrupt—in some spiritual traditions, a sign of the particular holiness of the deceased. Her feast is celebrated on April 24.

ROME

Marcella

One of the first persons to establish a monastic community in Rome was the widow Marcella. Born in 325 CE, she first learned of the ascetic movement in 340, when some Egyptian monks visited Rome. Soon she founded her own monastic community in her palace on the Aventine Hill, a wealthy area of Rome. Tradition places the Basilica of Santa Sabina on the ruins of this compound of homes. Principia joined Marcella's community. They quickly became close friends and constant companions.

Marcella fasted moderately, abstained from meat, and

seldom drank wine. She rarely went out in public and avoided visiting other noble women. However, her monastery hosted many visitors who wanted to deepen their knowledge of scripture and to learn of the ascetic way. Marcella privately visited the basilicas dedicated to the apostles and martyrs for prayer.

Marcella's younger sister, Asella,[20] lived in solitude in the family compound that was Marcella's monastic community. Paula the Elder,[21] a member of another wealthy and aristocratic Roman family, was a frequent visitor and became a keen student of scripture under Marcella. Later, Paula's daughter, Eustochium,[22] was raised and trained in Marcella's community until she left with her widowed mother for Bethlehem.

Fabiola, a young married aristocrat, was also a member of Marcella's circle of friends and followers. Initially, Fabiola flitted between ascetic observance and active participation in Roman social life. She divorced her philandering husband, but later married another man who was just as unfaithful. She eventually left him without bothering to obtain a divorce and joined the ranks of the penitents.[23] Fabiola, after reconciliation with the Christian community, sold her estates and devoted her immense wealth and service to the poor. With the help of a friend, Pammachius, she founded a hospital and helped care for the sick there. In 395, she visited Paula in Bethlehem and settled into an austere, solitary life nearby. She was particularly eager to study scripture, and her sharp mind kept Paula busy. Returning to Rome, Fabiola established a hospice for pilgrims at the port of the city. Jerome wrote of Fabiola, "Was there a naked or bedridden person who was not clothed with garments supplied by her? Were there ever any in want to whom she failed to give a quick and unhesitating supply? Even Rome was not wide enough for her pity."[24] She died in 399.

Marcella and Principia were astute students of the Bible. Marcella knew Greek and gained a reputation for her detailed, literal biblical exegesis. She had a fondness for "scholarly disquisitions into obscure words and phrases."[25] Strong-minded and educated,[26] Marcella debated significant points of scripture with Jerome,[27] who later credited her with much of his own learning. Jerome introduced Marcella's community to the controversial idea of studying Hebrew in order to read the Hebrew Bible in the original language.

After Jerome's departure for Jerusalem, Marcella became the person whom many, including priests, sought out for debate and discussion of scripture.[28] Marcella mentored Melania the Elder,[29] Paula and her daughter Eustochium, and Sophronia.

Marcella considered Origen a heretic.[30] She debated with his followers and challenged them to come to Rome and refute her. She gave evidence to Pope Anastasius that Origen's writings were corrupting Christians. Origen's writings were condemned in Egypt, and Pope Anastasius convened a synod that anathematized his teachings.

During the conquest of Rome in 410, Goth soldiers broke into the monastery seeking gold. After they were beaten, their assailants escorted Marcella and Principia to the basilica dedicated to Paul.[31] Marcella and Principia remained there until it was safe to return home. Several months later, Marcella died. Her feast day is January 31.

Lea

With the success and attraction of Marcella's monastic community, other communities began to spring up around Rome. Lea, a widow and friend of Marcella, established and led one of these communities. Lea was from a prominent family and nobility but left all this when she founded her community.

Lea wore simple, rough clothing, prayed during the night, and was renowned for teaching the monastic way more by example than by words. Jerome wrote to Marcella from the Holy Land because of her distress at not being able to perform the last offices for Lea.

Marcellina

Marcellina, the sister of Saint Ambrose, also established herself as an ascetic around 352 CE, living in the family home in Rome. Rome continued to see small and large monastic communities established and evolve over the years. None were formally organized, instead each crafting their own rule, until the reign of Charlemagne in the ninth century when monasteries began adopting the *Rule of Saint Benedict*.

PALESTINE

Bethlehem

The region around Bethlehem had inviting terrain for desert ascetics and small communities of believers. Pilgrims frequented the city to visit the holy sites, especially the alleged birthplace of Jesus. Pilgrims would then also seek out the desert solitaries for spiritual counsel and blessings. Monastic communities for women and men were established in and near Bethlehem.

Paula the Elder

Born in 347 CE, Paula the Elder was a wealthy aristocrat in Roman society. She was required to host receptions for many of her social class, which she did without becoming attached to or enamored of her prominent position. Paula was known for her gentle sense of humor. She and her husband, Toxotius, were the happily married parents of five children, including Eustochium.

Paula was a friend of Marcella and often visited her monastery for prayer and scripture study. Paula became proficient in her study of scripture and a scholar in her own right. She and Eustochium favored the allegorical approach to scripture, seeking moral and spiritual edification. Paula mastered Hebrew so well that she could chant the psalms without a hint of an accent.

Paula and Toxotius personally saw to the distribution of their wealth to the needy. They were kind and considerate, especially toward the poor and powerless. Paula's charity caused some concern and public scandal: her generosity led some to believe that her children would be left destitute. She was thirty-two when Toxotius died, leaving her grief-stricken.

Paula deeply loved her children, and they returned her affection. Jerome describes her parting for Cyprus in 385 CE with only her daughter, Eustochium. The others were well provided for from her estate and would stay with family. Yet her heart was torn, and an inner battle raged as she followed her inner call to leave Rome.

Paula and her party sailed for Cyprus where they met Jerome's party. Together they traveled on to Antioch and began visiting sites in the Holy Land. They traveled to Alexandria in Egypt and then ventured into the Nitrian desert to visit the ascetics. Eventually Paula and her entourage settled in Bethlehem. She stayed in a simple hostel for three years while she built her first monastery, consisting of numerous cells, monastic buildings, and a guesthouse.

Paula had a reputation for being authentic and down to earth. She did not draw attention to herself; she was comfortable to be who she was. Paula was known for her simplicity of person, interaction, friendship, and lifestyle. To avoid scandal, she never ate with men. She bathed rarely, slept on the hard ground on a mat of goat's hair, and observed a regular schedule of prayer. She was known for being patient with the frailties of others.

Paula immersed herself in scripture; it was often her consolation in difficult situations. She continued to debate fine points of translation and meaning with Jerome, although he found her irritating yet helpful in his work on the Vulgate.

She lived with the disapproval and anger of her social class for her way of life and for her refusal to give special attention to upper-class visitors.

Paula built three monasteries for women and one for men. She took pastoral responsibility for the women, Jerome for the men. Her communities contained noble, middle, and lower-class women. Each community of women worked at making clothing and ate separately but gathered for prayer. They prayed the psalms at dawn, the third, sixth, and ninth hours, in the evening and at midnight. Each spent time every day memorizing scripture, beginning with the psalms. For Sunday Mass, they walked to the nearby Church of the Nativity, built upon the cave where Jesus was supposed to have been born.

In her pastoral care, Paula worked to erase class distinctions. She worked hard with individuals to resolve conflicts, improve relationships, and guide them toward deeper monastic observance. Ultimately, she sought to develop each woman's ability to live the interior life and to build a monastic community of relationships that supported this.

Desiring to be poor as Jesus was, Paula continued to give her wealth away to the poor, and then began to take out loans in order to continue her giving. She died in 404 after a lingering illness. With her death, Paula left her daughter Eustochium with extensive debts.

Paula's funeral was held in the Church of the Nativity. Her body was carried on a bier by the local bishops. The mourning began with several days of chanting the psalms in Greek, Latin, Syriac, and Hebrew. Hundreds attended her funeral, monastics as well as the poor. Paula is buried beneath this church. Her feast day is January 26.

Eustochium and Paula the Younger

When Eustochium took over leadership of the monastic community, membership numbered around fifty. She was a quieter leader than Paula. Like her mother, Eustochium was a scripture scholar with a strong mastery of Hebrew. She paid off her mother's debts and got the community in sound financial shape before her death in 419 CE.

Her niece, Paula the Younger, was born around 400 CE to Laeta, the sister of Eustochium. She was sent at a very young age to Bethlehem to be raised by her aunt, Eustochium. Her education was directed, mostly in the classical style, by Jerome in the form of instructions. As a young child she was allowed several toys but otherwise was kept from the general society. She was to live a simple life but afforded a good education, including Greek, a subject normally only taught to sons. With the death of Eustochium, Paula the Younger, only eighteen years old, was named the next leader of the monastic community.

Jerusalem: The Mount of Olives

Jerusalem, long a bustling and busy city, played host to many Christian pilgrims wishing to visit the holy sites. Some would stay for a few days; others remained for months or years. Pilgrims desired to relive the life of Jesus by visiting the sites and walking the path where Jesus may have been, and spending time in prayer at each of these sites. Helena, the mother of Emperor Constantine, influenced the pilgrim tradition with her claim to have discovered the significant places of Jesus's life and ministry. Hermits and ascetics abounded, and monastic communities sprang up. Many individuals and monastic communities extended hospitality to the pilgrims flocking to Jerusalem.

Melania the Elder

Born around 341 CE, Melania was a Roman citizen of Spanish origin and daughter of the consul Marcellinus. At around age fourteen, Melania married a high-ranking member of the Valerii clan and resided among the aristocracy of Rome. She was widowed in 364 CE at age twenty-two. Two of Melania's three children soon followed their father in death. Melania was active in the ascetic circle of Rome centered around Marcella, devoting much of her time to the ascetic practices of prayer, fasting, study of the word, and good works.

In 372, Melania decided, as was customary, to go on a pilgrimage to Egypt to learn from the desert ascetics. She never intended to return to Rome. Melania made her plans secretly because the Emperor Valens[32] would have forbidden her to go and might have attempted to force her into another arranged marriage in order to maintain his base of power and to keep her wealth within the aristocratic circle. She placed her surviving son, Publicola, under guardianship in Rome so that he could continue his education and prepare for his place in the aristocracy. When her family discovered her plans, they tried unsuccessfully to detain and dissuade her.

Loading all her movable property onto a ship, Melania sailed for Alexandria, Egypt. Many women and children of her household joined her. Upon arriving, Melania sold all her possessions and went into the desert to the mountain of Nitria. She met with some of the church fathers: Pambo, Arisisus, Serapion the Great, Paphnutius of Scete, Isidore the Confessor, and Bishop Dioscourus of Hermopolis. Melania spent six months visiting monastic settlements in Egypt and learning more about the monastic way of life. While with Abba Pambo, Melania tried to give him a basket containing 300 pounds of silver, but he refused it. She in return was given the gift of the last basket Abba Pambo made before his death.

With the continued christological controversies,[33] a persecution broke out in 373, and many monks were banished from their monasteries. Many chose to go to the countryside of Palestine. Melania went with them and gave them financial support. When they first arrived in Palestine, Melania would dress in the evening as a slave in order to bring them

provisions. The consul of Palestine, upon learning that someone was assisting the banished men, arrested Melania with
the intent of "blackening"[34] her reputation and in hope of col-
lecting a bribe. When Melania confronted the consul with
her identity and position in society, he let her go and gave her
unhindered freedom to meet with these monks.

Melania built a monastery for fifty women on the Mount
of Olives in Jerusalem and lived there for twenty-seven years.
Her days were spent in prayer, work with the poor, hospitality toward pilgrims, and the study of scripture. Male teachers
praised her for her command of Greek, Latin, and Hebrew,
acknowledging that she could ask questions of interpretation
that they themselves were unable to answer.

She "received those who turned up in Jerusalem for the
sake of a vow, bishops, monks, and virgins," edifying all who
visited her monastery.[35] Among her more famous guests, in
385 CE, were Jerome and Paula, who would model their own
monastic communities on Melania's. Melania supported
Evagrius of Pontus[36] through his time of personal crisis when
he fell in love yet felt called to remain celibate. After instructing him in the monastic life, she sent him to Egypt to study
with the desert fathers there. In a letter Evagrius sent her from
Egypt, he commends her for being a "beautiful example" for
all who seek to overcome temptation and sin.

Melania built a monastery for men near her own community. Rufinus of Aquileia[37] developed a school and scripto-
rium, and the monasteries supported themselves by copying
manuscripts. Due to the large numbers of manuscripts, the
monastics flourished in a learned environment. Melania was
deeply involved in local church matters, including the schisms
over Paulinus[38] and over the divinity of the Holy Spirit. She
worked to restore unity, especially among monastics.

Melania used her wealth to build monasteries and
churches, provide hospitality to refugees and pilgrims, and
make provision for prisoners. Palladius tells us that she

lavished so much wealth in her godly zeal, as if she were ablaze with fire, that the residents of Persia, not I should do the reporting. No one in either the east or the west, the north or the south, failed to benefit from her good works…for twenty-seven years she offered hospitality; at her own expense, she assisted churches, monasteries, guests, and prisons…she persevered in her hospitality to such an extent that she did not keep a span of earth, nor pulled by longing for her son, did she separate herself from the love of Christ.[39]

Melania influenced a circle of men whose writings would become highly influential in the formation of Christian theology. She was perceived as mature in the spiritual journey and a capable theologian in her own right. In a letter to Sulpicius Severus (author of *The Life of St. Martin of Tours*), Paulinus of Nola wrote,

A woman of more elevated rank, she loftily cast herself down to a humble way of life, so that as a strong member of the weak sex she might censure indolent men, so that as a rich person appropriating poverty, and as a noble person adopting humility, she might confound people of both sexes.[40]

Learning that her married granddaughter, Melania the Younger, had decided to pursue the ascetic life, Melania the Elder returned to Rome in 400 CE, when she was sixty years old. While with her family, Melania the Elder worked to convert several members to Christianity, and she inspired others to become ascetics or monastics. Despite resistance from senatorial families, Melania sold her remaining real estate. Upon returning to Jerusalem and giving away the last of her wealth, Melania the Elder died.

Melania was renowned for her generosity and for her scholarship. Paulinus writes of her:

> Now know that there is such power of God in that member of the weak sex, that woman who finds restoration in fasting, repose in prayer, bread in the Word, clothing in rags. Her hard couch (it is a cloak and a patchwork quilt on the ground) is made soft by her scholarly work, because her delight in reading mitigates the insult of the inflexible bed, and it is rest to her holy soul to keep vigil in the Lord.[41]

Palladius writes,

> She was very learned and a lover of literature. She turned night into day by going through every writing of the ancient commentators, three million lines of Origen, and two hundred fifty thousand lines of Gregory, Stephen, Pierius, Basil, and other excellent men. And she did not merely glance through them casually, but laboring over them, she read each work seven or eight times. Therefore she could be freed from "knowledge falsely called" [1 Tim 6:20] and to take flight by the influence of the books, making herself a spiritual bird, passing over to Christ in good hopes.[42]

At Melania the Elder's death, her daughter-in-law Albina assumed leadership of the monastic community.

Albina

Born into a wealthy Roman family in the early 360s CE, Albina married Valerius Publicola. After her husband's death she journeyed with her daughter and son-in-law (Melania the Younger and Pinianus) to Sicily. Three years later the family moved near Thagaste, in northern Africa, and stayed for seven years. Around 417 Albina and Melania traveled to Palestine where she remained until her death around 431.

Albina, although oftentimes overshadowed in history by her more famous mother and daughter, was an important part of the Christian movement of the early fifth century. She wrote at least sixty-nine letters to Augustine of Hippo. He, in turn, mentions Albina in several of his letters to other prominent leaders. She was connected with Jerome, Paulinus of Nola, and Pelagius.

Melania the Younger

Melania the Younger was born in 383 CE into aristocracy and was raised amid Marcella's Roman ascetic circle. Her biographer describes her as having a heart burning with divine fire. Melania was married to Pinianus in 397, but she preferred a life focused on God. Pinianus felt obligated to have two children to carry on the family name; they were born shortly afterward.[43] Melania nearly died with the birth of her second child, and Pinianus reluctantly agreed that they would live as brother and sister. They dedicated their time and wealth to the Christian movement. Both children subsequently died, but Melania remained adamant that she would bear no more.[44]

Melania and Pinianus began to simplify their lives and withdraw from such trappings of their social class as refined foods, silk clothing, and gold. They dedicated their time to visiting the sick and extended hospitality to foreigners and made provision for their travels. They visited prisoners, the mines in which slaves and prisoners were forced to work, and places where the marginalized lived, giving generously to free those imprisoned for debt and providing for those they could not free. Eventually, they began to sell off their possessions in order to continue their charity for the needy and the churches.

Pinianus's brother Severus, as well as the senate, tried to intervene in order to take away their wealth, but Melania managed to outsmart them. She went to her friend, Serena, the daughter-in-law of the Emperor Honorius, bearing gifts of ornaments, silks, and crystal drinking glasses. Serena, upon hearing her story, intervened with the emperor, who decreed that Melania and Pinianus were free to sell all their possessions throughout the empire. This was unusual because most emperors wanted all imperial wealth to remain within the royal family.

Melania and Pinianus began to give their riches away in bulk. They purchased several islands and hermitages around Constantinople for ascetics and supported them. They gave away their remaining silk garments to the churches and monasteries for use on the altars.

Melania and Pinianus decided they wanted to leave Rome, with its pressures and expectations of them as aristocrats. They traveled first to Nola, where they visited Bishop Paulinus, his wife, Therasia, and their monastic community. Then they traveled on to Sicily in 407 CE. In 410, soon after they had sold all their estates in Italy and Spain, Alaric invaded and conquered the region.

Melania and Pinianus sailed for Africa in 410 CE and sold all their African estates. They endowed many of the monastic communities, who then lived off the interest without touching the principle. Saint Augustine mentored and guided them.

Melania and Pinianus decided to make the small, poor town of Thagaste their home. They wanted to be near Bishop Alypius, Saint Augustine's friend and a scripture scholar. Melania spent hours in study and debate. While in Thagaste, they founded and endowed a monastery for women and for men.

As their wealth finally began to diminish, Melania also began to feel free enough from the burden of her wealth to begin a more contemplative life. She began severe fasts, remained for lengthy periods in solitude, and studied. Her biographer, Gerontius, tells us that Melania wrote elegantly and faultlessly in little notebooks. She mentally decided how much she should write each day, how much in the Canonical Books [of scripture] she should read, and how much in the collections of homilies. After she had had her fill of these writings, she went through the lives of the Fathers as if she were eating a cake.[45]

After spending seven years in Africa, Melania and Pinianus visited Alexandria before arriving in 417 on the Mount of Olives. It seems she informally took over leadership of the double community, although Albina, her mother, led the women and Pinianus led the men's community until his death in 432. Melania wrote the rule for the community, establishing liturgical and ascetical practices as well as overseeing the spiritual growth of the women. Even when Melania appointed another woman superior of the community after the death of Albina in 420, she remained a potent force. Melania had a powerful and exuberant personality. She was strong-willed, zealous, and determined. Although she denied she was the leader, she clearly led.

Melania and Pinianus went on pilgrimage to the desert of Egypt in 419, visiting the ammas and abbas there. Upon return, Melania arranged for a water supply for the monastery and moved into the new, more reclusive cell her mother built for the two of them. She rarely saw anyone other than Albina, Pinianus, and her cousin Paula the Younger. When apart, Melania and Paula corresponded freely—a frequent topic was the importance of humility for an aristocratic ascetic.

Melania remained a recluse for fourteen years. She lived in a cell with her mother and maintained limited contact with the other members of the community. However, she would leave her cell to engage visiting scholars in discussion. She also continued expansion of the monastery complex. Albina and Melania disagreed over Melania's tendencies toward austere fasting and other observances—a disagreement that was never resolved.

Melania read the Hebrew and Christian scriptures completely three to four times each year. The women continued the tradition of copying elegant and accurate texts, sacred and secular. Melania copied much of what she wanted to read but was also able to borrow books; the community had a worthwhile library.

She exhorted others to follow her example and to divest themselves of their wealth. Many turned their estates over to her, and she arranged for the wise distribution of the proceeds.

The community prayed together several times each day. They prayed in anticipation of dawn, an office that consisted of three psalms, three readings, and fifteen antiphons as the sun rose. They prayed together again at the third, sixth, and ninth hours.

While living in extreme poverty herself, Melania traveled freely in wealthy and powerful circles, comfortable with her high profile and simple life. Empresses, senators, and aristocrats were within her circle of influence. Melania built several churches and monasteries in addition to her own on the Mount of Olives.

Melania went to Constantinople to visit an uncle who was still a nonbeliever, in the hope of converting him. There she met with the Emperor Valentinian III[46] and Empress Eudoxia. Melania convinced the empress to visit the Holy Land on pilgrimage, and Melania met her in Sidon.

Melania died during the Christmas season of 439 CE. Paula, members of both communities, and several prominent people were with her at death. Many of the ascetics from the surrounding region came to join the monastic community in chanting the psalms throughout the night and buried Melania the following morning.

GAUL

Caesaria

In Arles, several monastic communities of women thrived. Around 500 CE, Bishop Caesarius began the construction of a monastery for his sister Caesaria and her community outside the city walls near the old Gallo-Roman cemetery called the Aliscamps. Caesaria had been living and studying the monastic life in Marseille, another location of many monasteries of diverse membership. When invading Franks and Burgundians destroyed the first monastery building in 508–9, Caesarius began construction of a second compound (this time within the city walls) with a cloister to protect the women from physical harm. Later, such an enclosure would be associated with a spirituality that valued withdrawal from society. Abbess Caesaria would have the keys to the lock, which would have been on the inside of the door.[47]

Caesaria's community, called Saint John of Arles, spent much of their time studying scripture and supporting themselves by copying manuscripts. The rule—written by Bishop Caesarius, brother of the Elder Caesaria[48]—provided for the recitation of eighteen psalms during the night office, six psalms during each of the day offices, and scripture readings during vigils. Each member memorized the Psalter, so that their hearts would be transformed by their immersion in the scriptures. Bishop Caesarius considered the authority of the abbess to be so central to the monastic observance that his rule forbids any abbess ever to transfer the authority of her office to any bishop. The pope backed him up in writing.

The monastery gave as much of its wealth to the poor as it could, balanced by the awareness that it must maintain an endowment for its own protection. Wealthier monasteries enjoyed greater protection than poorer ones.

In 524, Caesarius completed the construction and dedicated the Basilica of Saint Mary, providing a burial place for the members of Caesaria's community. Caesaria died shortly thereafter and was buried under this basilica, and Caesaria the Younger succeeded her as abbess. The community flourished in numbers and wealth under her leadership. She freely shared the wisdom of her way of life and Rule; many of her letters survive. The younger Caesaria disapproved of excessive devotions and severe fasts, exhorting those who were displaying such tendencies.

Under the fourth abbess, Rusticula, the monastery was rebuilt at the east angle of the city walls, near the Tour des Morgues. Although several new buildings would be built in the course of history, Caesaria's community continued in existence until the French Revolution in 1789.

Radegunde

Radegunde, born in 525 CE, was the reluctant wife of Clothar I and a queen of the Franks. Radegunde used her personal wealth to build hospitals and minister to the poor during her marriage. She left her husband in 550 upon learning that he had ordered the murder of her brother. Arriving in Noyon, she demanded that the bishop, Medard, consecrate her a nun. He instead made Radegunde a deacon since she was still married.[49]

Radegunde made a pilgrimage to Tours and then settled at her estate at Saix in the region of Poitou. She lived there for several years, devoting her time to prayer and service to the poor. She followed a simple vegetarian diet and soon developed a reputation as a contemplative and mystic.

Perhaps as a final settlement on the dissolution of their marriage, Radegunde was endowed with the means to establish a monastery of women at Poitiers sometime between 552 and 559. Her monastery adopted the *Rule of Arles*—a copy given to her by the younger Caesaria. Radegunde habitually performed the most menial domestic tasks around the monastery, in defiance of her highborn station in life.

Radegunde had a talent for pastoral care and spiritual direction. She studied and preached daily, as well as dedicating time to private prayer, and was well versed in the writings of early church leaders. She served as spiritual mother while refusing appointment as abbess; Richeldix was probably the first abbess. One of Radegunde's early followers, Agnes, served later.

Radegunde venerated the relics of saints and collected many from around the Roman Empire. She believed that they linked her with the saints in continuous meditation. Sometime in 567 or 568, she was able to secure a relic of the true cross.

Radegunde died August 13, 587. Her death was unexpected and the cause remains unknown. She was buried outside the cloister, as was the custom of the day.

Chapter Seven

DESERT STORIES WITH A MORAL

Most of us have grown up with familiar family stories: our oral tradition. They are told over and over, remembering the colorful, poignant, even troubling members and events of our families and communities. Stories are preserved and told among friends and families and religious communities. These stories are remembered because they touch us deeply. They tell us something of who we are and of where we have been. Stories unpack the mystery of the present and give us guidance into the future. We pass particular stories on because, having shaken something awake within us, we desire to share this new awareness and insight with others. We want to remember the lesson learned. Stories contain and sustain our cultural values; they assist in passing on the traditions of our families, faith communities, and monasteries.

So, too, stories were told in the desert and passed among faith communities to instruct and encourage as well as to confound and confuse, especially for those seekers and students of the desert whose confidence was ill placed.

I begin with two stories of similar theme, although each has its own origin.

THE HOLY DRUNKEN WOMAN[1]

Abba Daniel visited the Upper Thebaid on the Feast of Abba Apollo, visiting first the monastic community of men and then the monastic community of women. The community of three hundred women was called the Monastery of Abba Jeremiah. The women "violated" the tradition of not permitting men in their monastery[2] in order to welcome a particularly venerated and beloved elder of the desert. In the tradition of desert hospitality, these monastic women welcomed Abba Daniel and his companion into their monastery chapel and washed their feet. The women then blessed themselves with the water used, sought a blessing, and then a word of teaching or exhortation.

It was when the women sought a wise word from Abba Daniel—a common theme of desert stories—that the scene shifts to an anonymous member of the women's monastery who stayed away from the rest of the community. Here, this anonymous nun, believed to be drunk, was asleep in the forecourt of the church, wearing rags that were in shreds. Abba Daniel asks the amma who this nun was, and she responds, "She's a drunk and we don't know what to do with her. We're afraid to take the responsibility of throwing her out of the monastery, but if we let her stay, she demoralizes the sisters."

The community then redirected Abba Daniel and his companion to their refectory for a shared meal. They served the men simple vegetarian fare while the women ate well. When Abba Daniel inquired about this seeming disparity and violation of hospitality, the amma responded, "You are a monk and I served you a monk's food. We, however, are novices and we ate novice's food." By example, the women exalted the venerable teacher by lowering themselves in an odd paradox.

As they were leaving, Abba Daniel again inquired about the "drunken nun" who was found sleeping by the toilets. The men hid themselves so they could watch this nun. As the monastery retired for sleep, the woman arose and stood in a position of tearful supplication or prostrated herself in contrition. Whenever a nun came out to use the toilet, she would throw herself on the ground and snore.

Abba Daniel called the amma who joined him in observing this behavior. With tearful repentance, the leader confronted herself with her own history of treating this nun poorly. Abba Daniel saw this nun's total disregard for her reputation. Her humility in not wanting to be known for her holiness meant that she was indeed the wise elder among them.

When the drunken nun realized that she has been discovered, she cleverly stole Abba Daniel's cowl and staff and disappeared into the desert. Abba Daniel and the amma declared the drunken nun to be one of God's hidden servants.

THE NUN WHO FEIGNED MADNESS

If anyone among you seems to be wise in this world, let her become a fool in order to be wise.

1 Cor 3:18

From Palladius[3] we learn of a women's monastery at Tabennisi[4] in Egypt where a member feigned madness and demon-possession. She was treated with contempt and the nuns avoided her company. This "mad nun" voluntarily worked at the most menial jobs in the kitchen. She wore a rag on her head when other members cropped their hair short and wore a cowl. She ate only scraps and leftovers. She was never angry, never grumbled, rarely spoke—all amid contemptuous treatment. She was insulted, cursed, and loathed by her fellow nuns.

An angel appeared to Abba Piteroum, another venerated desert ascetic, inviting him to meet someone holier than he. The angel sent him to Tabennisi with a challenge: *This woman is continually mistreated by her community and yet never takes her heart off God while our Venerable Abba dwells in his cell yet wanders about the cities in his mind.*[5] This is a common theme throughout desert teachings, including the Sayings of Amma Syncletica.

Abba Piteroum arrived for his angelic lesson at the women's monastery, seeking this holy woman whom the nuns referred to as *touched*. She resisted meeting the holy man but was physically forced into his presence. He immediately recognized her as spiritually mature by an intuition and knowing of the heart. He fell to his feet, seeking her blessing. She responded by falling to her feet and seeking his blessing. They each vied to express their humility. The nuns were aghast.

Abba Piteroum declared the "touched nun" to be the community's true spiritual mother. The nuns recognized the truth of his words and immediately began to confess their mistreatment of this unknown amma and elder. Now elevated to "venerable," she could not tolerate the place of honor and disappeared from the community. "Where she went, where she hid away, or how she died, nobody knew."

Why Were These Two Stories Preserved and Shared?

What was your initial reaction? Did you laugh? Were you disturbed or even appalled? Did you roll your eyes and wonder why anyone would have told this story?

"The Holy Drunken Woman" and "The Nun Who Feigned Madness" speak to us of the paradox of ultimate detachment, a paradox because it seems that their pursuit of profound interior freedom caused disruption for others. These women speak to us of the paradox of letting go of care and concern for our reputations, especially when a spiritual practice that could assist my own interior freedom and self-awareness in pursuit of the Holy Other may cause legitimate scandal to others. These ammas certainly speak to us of the myriad ways God is found outside our concept of "normal."

These women remind us that our teachers and mentors may come in the form of Balaam's Ass (Num 23–24)—or a holy drunken woman or a woman who feigns madness. Indeed, our troubling family members and neighbors call forth the strength of compassion, steadfastness, and vision in unforeseen ways. Sometimes we successfully bring out our best selves; sometimes our worst self comes out. These stories clearly teach the paradox of who was actually troubled: the woman or the community? Each amma who was the focus of the story expressed outwardly disturbing behavior but is revealed to have a pure heart intent only on God. The community of nuns outwardly expressed conformity and even appropriateness (not always the same thing) but inward misbehavior and even wickedness.

We are presented with a paradox that does not allow an easy answer: what appears to be wickedness of behavior does not always mean wickedness of heart. Where we may find this hard to believe, the Bible reminds us that "God's ways are not our ways." This paradox is a teaching moment: what appears as "bad" is shown to be "good." What is in us—our purity of heart, or the lack therein—is exposed.

As with all good stories, we are not allowed easy answers to difficult questions. Paradox lives on. Discernment is required. Self-awareness is needed in order to understand the power behind story and why we repeat them in our dining rooms. The mad nun and drunken woman confront us: Who are our teachers? From whom are we willing to learn? At whose feet do we sit to receive the wisdom of desert cell and monastery? What do we do when presumptions, prejudices, and expectations are thwarted? How do we discern? With whom do we discern? Who are our wise elders?

MARIA OF MESOPOTAMIA

Maria[6] was orphaned when she was seven years old and went to live with her uncle, a desert ascetic named Abraham. Her uncle built a cell for her attached to his hermitage with a window between the two cells and arranged for her inheritance to be distributed for the care of other orphans. He taught her the Psalter[7] and other scriptures, how to pray, and to live the life of a desert ascetic, aided by his friend archdeacon Ephraim, another ascetic. She soon had cultivated an inner quiet and especially a heart of charity. She held fast to the teachings of her uncle, and her uncle prayed daily that his niece would be spared the temptations of the devil.

Having lived this way of life for twenty years, temptation arrived in the form of a so-called monk. This unnamed monk came to meet with her uncle for spiritual direction but became enamored of this unseen niece. For a year he tried to talk to her of "love" and eventually her heart and spirit wore down by his persistence. The day came when he approached, and she agreed to leave her cell and sleep with him. He then disappeared.

Overwhelmed with grief for what she had done and believing herself to be beyond repentance and God's mercy, Maria fled to another city, changed her name, and became a prostitute.

Her uncle Abraham had a series of vivid dreams that revealed what became of his beloved niece, Maria. For two years he prayed for her return, not knowing where she had gone. He asked a friend to make inquiries as to his niece's whereabouts. When the friend found out where she was, Abraham asked his friend to borrow a soldier's attire and a horse so Abraham could go after her unrecognized.

Arriving in the city, Abraham located the brothel where Maria lived and presented himself as a customer. He asked for Maria and paid for her time and a sumptuous meal with wine. Maria dined with her uncle without recognizing him. As the story goes, his willingness to break his fast of many years to eat meat and drink wine is considered an act of profound love. Mercy and love were more important than the strict regimen of an ascetic. Then Maria takes him to her chamber, and only then does her uncle reveal himself to her. He expresses both his grief that she did not trust him to tell him what had happened, and that she had fled into this terrible life. His was an expression of deep love for her and an admonishment to never reject the mercy and love of God. As Abraham said to Maria, "For who is without sin but God alone? It is not new to fall. What is wrong is to lie down when we've fallen."

Maria and Abraham returned to their cells in the desert, and in order to protect her, Abraham took the outer cell and she the inner one. She resumed her ascetical practices, lamenting her fall and praying in gratitude for her deliverance. As a sign that she had been reconciled to God, she received the gift of healing. Soon many were coming to her, and in praying for their needs, they were healed.

Her uncle, Abraham, died about ten years after her return. After another five years of faithful observance, Maria too went home to God.

Why Was This Story Preserved and Shared?

Maria, like many in the stories from the desert and monastic tradition, renounced all her material goods, severing ties with the world around her. Material goods are not bad in themselves, but rather the goal was interior freedom and detachment from earthly cares. As we know, with possessions come responsibilities.

Yet this was, at its core, a story of the fragility of our spiritual journey and the limitlessness of God's mercy and desire to forgive us. We are moved by the uncle's tender love for his niece and his willingness to stretch beyond his own comfort zone and even reputation to meet with Maria and invite her to return home. Nothing is beyond the love and mercy of God.

Maria's story, like several others, is about avoiding the pitfall of despair, an expression of pride that denies the possibility of forgiveness.

Early Christians were not literalists. They always looked for the deeper meaning of stories.[8] With Maria and her uncle, Abraham, they recognized an echo of our salvation story. Abraham was seen as Christ, God-become-human, who came to save us from sin.

MARY THE EGYPTIAN

Mary[9] was born in Egypt. At twelve years of age, she spurned her parents' care for her and left for Alexandria. By her own account, she became quite sexually aggressive, refusing offers of money for sexual favors. She gave them freely, supporting herself by begging and spinning thread from flax. Thus, Mary was not a prostitute but led a dissolute lifestyle for seventeen years.

One summer she noticed a large number of Egyptians and Libyans going down to the docks on the Mediterranean Sea. Curious, she stopped one of them and asked what was going on. He responded, "They are all going to Jerusalem for the Exaltation of the Holy Cross, which is to be celebrated there in a few days' time."[10] Intending to look for "more interesting lovers," she followed a group of handsome young men and slipped onto one of the boats with them. While sailing she slept with some and seduced others who were originally unwilling. By her own admission, Mary was successful in seducing men and was proud of it.

As the group traveled on to Jerusalem, Mary claimed to have seduced other pilgrims her group encountered. When the festival of the Exaltation of the Holy Cross came around, at dawn Mary was busy looking for the next good-looking man to seduce. She noticed crowds walking toward the cathedral.[11] Curious, she pushed her way forward through the crowds to get to the front and see the wood of the cross on display for veneration. As she approached the threshold of the cathedral, while others were able to enter, a mysterious force did not allow her to go in. She tried several times, hiding herself amid a small crowd, but each time she attempted to enter, she was barred. An unexplained power repelled her.

Exhausted by her efforts, Mary stood in a corner of the forecourt. The Holy Spirit touched her heart and convinced Mary of her sin, both against her own humanity and that of others. She wept and wept from deep within. Looking up through her tears, she saw an image of the Blessed Virgin Mary. She recognized the Virgin, confessed her awareness of the Christian message of salvation, and beseeched the Virgin to receive her confession and allow her to enter the church and venerate the cross. Mary also asked the Virgin to both guarantee her promise to never sin again and guide her in turning her life around. This prayer of Mary the Egyptian to the Blessed Virgin Mary is one of the earliest stories of someone seeking the Virgin's intercession for help.

With new faith burning within her and "receiving some assurance from some sure source, and trusting in of the mercy of heart of the mother of God,"[12] she stepped out and joined another group entering the church. This time she was able to pass through and, falling to the ground, worshiped the wood of the cross. Eventually she returned to the courtyard and again spoke to the image of the Virgin, prepared to fulfill her promise to the Virgin: "Lead me wherever you please; lead me to salvation, teach me what is true, and go before me in the way of repentance." Having said this, she heard a far-off voice tell her to cross over the Jordan River, where she would find rest. Taking three loaves of bread she left Jerusalem on a road leading to the Jordan.

Mary wandered the Judean desert alone for forty-seven years, praying for the forgiveness of God and for those she had harmed. Like other desert ascetics, she prayed continuously, including the psalms, and pondered God's mercy. Unlike most desert ascetics, her clothing became rags, and she became naked. One day she saw someone in the distance— apparently, a first for her—and turned away. Walking some distance, she glanced back and noticed the person was following her. She picked up her pace and began running but so did this person.

Finally, he caught up with her and called out. He asked for a blessing and wise word (what seekers wanted from a desert ascetic). She turned and ran away. He chased after her, calling out. She kept running and he pursued. Finally, she crossed a dry creek bed. The two stood on opposite sides, she with her back to him. She rebuked him by name, demanding his cloak to cover herself. Surprised, this strange pursuer bundled and threw her his cloak. He approached as she covered herself and knelt before her. Mary knelt, called him by name, and since he was a priest, she insisted that he should provide the blessing. As they had not met before, Abba Zossima decided her knowledge of his identity must be by the power of the Holy Spirit, and saying this to her, insisted she give the blessing as the one closer to God. Mary acquiesced, praying, "Blessed is God who cares for the salvation of souls," and Zossima responded with "Amen."

Mary was emaciated from years of fasting and dwelling under the heat of the desert sun. Her rags failed to cover her, her naked skin was dark as if scorched by the sun, and she had shoulder-length white hair. After telling Abba Zossima her story, she went on to explain that for the first seventeen years in the desert, she endured significant inner struggles, which, in her words, was like wrestling with wild beasts. Powerful memories of enticing food and wine, memories of wild parties and lewd songs, of seducing men, haunted her. During these struggles she would remember the promise of faithfulness she had made before the image of the Virgin and implored her help with her soul's affliction.[13] A light would appear, surrounding her, and again Mary would know peace.

Mary sent Abba Zossima away with a blessing, requesting that he never tell others about her until after her death, and asking him to return the following year on Holy Thursday.[14] She requested they meet at the Jordan River, and that Abba Zossima bring the consecrated bread and wine for her—the first since she departed into the desert.

The following year, Mary departed the desert for the Jordan River. As there was no boat available, Mary "signed the water with the sign of the cross and crossed over, walking on water" and met Abba Zossima who, as she had requested, brought her the Eucharist. She requested he recite the Holy Creed[15] and the Lord's Prayer before giving her the Eucharist. She refused his request to stay with her for a while and learn from her and receive the blessing of her company. Instead she requested that he return in a year's time to the dried creek where they had initially met.

Thus, a year later Abba Zossima went into the desert to the place where they had first met and searched for her. He searched in vain in all directions along the dried creek bed until he found her lying dead, covered only in the tattered cloak he had given her when they first met, facing to the East with her hands folded. Weeping at his loss, Abba Zossima prayed "the appropriate psalms and then the prayer for the dead." Looking around, he wondered where and how he could bury her. Then he noticed that Mary had written in the dirt,

"Father Zossima, bury in this place the body of Mary the sinner, return me to the earth of which I am made, dust to dust, having prayed to the Lord for me, who died in the first day of the Egyptian month of Pharmuti called the fifth of the Ides of April by the Romans, on the same night as the Passion of the Lord after making her communion of the Divine and Mysterious Supper."[16]

As a lovely and fitting ending to her story, Abba Zossima tried to dig a grave for her body, but he didn't have any implement and the dirt was hard. Suddenly a lion appeared with a friendly expression on its face and, after he beseeched the creature for assistance, the lion began to dig a grave for Mary with its paws. Abba Zossima returned to his monastery, and for the first time told his story of meeting Amma Mary the Egyptian.

Mary is commemorated on April 1 in the Orthodox tradition and on the Fifth Sunday of Lent in the West.

Why Was This Story Preserved and Shared?

Mary the Egyptian's story became widely popular in the sixth century and remained so throughout the Middle Ages. The stories of several courtesans who gave up that lifestyle for a life dedicated to Jesus Christ were conflated into this one story. At times, especially in art, Mary the Egyptian was confused with Mary of Magdala, Jesus's companion, and the unnamed woman in Luke 7:36–39, who anoints Jesus's feet with her hair. She was portrayed wearing animal skins with hair down to her ankles (the new "John the Baptist") but then misidentified as Mary of Magdala. In the Middle Ages, Mary's story grew and expanded, and was retold and written down over the centuries. Her story was performed in plays.

This story resonated with Christians. It was a story of the deepest sin, turned by the love and mercy of Christ into the greatest glory. It reminded people that there was no sin that could not be turned into something good. Her story embodied the desert teaching on *penthos,* the gift of tears that cleanses the heart as well as *kenosis,* given the years she spent in the desert anguishing over those she harmed by her actions.

However, Mary's story also attracted listeners because it was a story of a women exercising great spiritual power: She knew Abba Zossima and his Abbot, John, by name without ever having met them. She knew what was going on in Abba Zossima's monastery without ever having visited. She walked on water and survived for years on a minimum of food and water. She wandered the desert safely, she knew the time of her death, and "arranged" for a lion to appear when needed to bury her.

PELAGIA THE PENITENT

In the city of Antioch lived a famous actress, Pelagia.[17] Publicly she was known as "Margaret," which means "pearl," due to the amount of jewelry she wore. A successful actress,[18] she spent hours on her personal grooming and attire, and her public display of jewelry announced her popularity and success.

Deacon James[19] of Edessa accompanied Bishop Nonnus of Heliopolis[20] to a gathering of eight bishops in Antioch. While conducting their business outside the doors of the church dedicated to the martyr Julianus, Pelagia rode by on her donkey, accompanied by several of her servants and members of the acting chorus. The scent of her perfume wafted through the air. She was elaborately dressed in gold, pearls, and precious stones. Her head was bare[21] and her limbs exposed. Her entourage played instruments and sang. She was a stunning beauty.

While many of the bishops looked away, Bishop Nonnus gazed at her until she was out of sight. "Isn't she lovely?" he asked of his fellow bishops. He went on to compare the hours Pelagia presumably spent adorning herself in preparation for a play in order to please her audience to the hours the bishops did or didn't spend preparing their souls for the Beloved Bridegroom.

The following day, a Sunday, Bishop Nonnus was preaching in church when Pelagia entered—having never entered a church before—and stood discreetly in a corner. She was shocked by what she heard but understood the truth of what the bishop was saying. She departed but sent one of her servants with a message to Bishop Nonnus requesting a meeting. Having perceived the truth of his message, she wanted to become a Christian.

Bishop Nonnus was reluctant to baptize her, concerned that she would simply return to her old way of life.[22] She again implored him for baptism: "I have looked so closely into my heart that I cannot find there any single good action. I know my sins and they are more than the sand upon the seashore: water like the sea is little compared to the extent of my sins. But I trust in your God."[23] Bishop Nonnus sent word to the bishop of Antioch to send a deaconess to train Pelagia in the teachings of Christianity. The senior deaconess, Romana,[24] arrived and, after Pelagia was baptized, anointed her with the chrism oils and the laying on of hands to receive the Holy Spirit. As was the custom at that time, she put on a white garment to be worn for the first eight days after baptism. Pelagia went to live with Romana and the other catechumens.[25]

When she was tempted to return to her old way of life, especially due to her strong sense of guilt, she would make the sign of the cross as she dismissed the thought (literally: "blew her breath at the demon tempting her"), and the guilt would depart. Three days after her baptism, Pelagia called for her servant and sent him to her rooms to inventory all she had possessed. When he returned with the list, Pelagia, with the deaconess Romana, called for Bishop Nonnus and presented him with the inventory list. She gave everything she owned to him. In turn, Bishop Nonnus called for the senior custodian of the church, ordered that all her goods be sold and the money distributed to the widows, orphans, and the poor. Pelagia then called for all her servants and set them free, giving each a gold collar, and exhorting them to become Christians as well.

On the night of the eighth day when, as a catechumen, she would normally take off the white garment and don regular clothing, Pelagia instead put on a tunic and breeches belonging to Bishop Nonnus, the "theft" of which he was not aware, and disappeared from the city of Antioch. She traveled to Jerusalem and built herself a cell on the Mount of Olives, where she lived in seclusion, dedicating herself to a life steeped in prayer. Probably to protect herself from those who might be tempted to attack her, Pelagia changed her name to the masculine form, Pelagius.

Somehow Bishop Nonnus knew what Pelagia had done. When Deacon James told Bishop Nonnus that he wanted to visit Jerusalem and pray at the holy sites, the bishop told him to ask for the monk "Pelagius" and visit him. Deacon James did so, knocking on her window (the cell was otherwise fully enclosed, much like a mausoleum). Not realizing the monk Pelagius was the actress Pelagia, he encountered "a face emaciated from much fasting with sunken eyes."[26] As was the custom in visiting desert ascetics and hermits, he hoped for a word that might deepen his relationship with God. When she asked why Deacon James sought her out, he said he was sent by Bishop Nonnus. She responded, "Tell him to pray for me, for he is a saint of God." She closed her window and resumed chanting the psalms.

As Deacon James continued his visits to monastic communities and holy sites, he discovered that the monk Pelagius was renowned and venerated. He was determined to visit this famous monk again, hoping for "some saving teaching." Arriving at her cell, he made several attempts to get the monk's attention but received no response. As he was about to leave, the Spirit nudged him to break open the window, and he saw that the venerable monk was dead. As others gathered with him, they gently removed the body to be anointed for proper burial and discovered that the monk Pelagius was a woman. A throng of monastics and believers joined in the burial procession, bearing lamps and candles, and singing hymns.

Discovering that Pelagius was the woman Pelagia, no one was surprised that a woman had lived such an austere life.

Why Was This Story Preserved and Shared?

Pelagia's story was popular in early Christianity, retold in many forms to the point that it took scholars some effort to tease out the historical persons from all the retellings of her story. It even has a pleasant shock value of a bishop who could freely enjoy the beauty of a woman, even a woman of ill repute, without needing to "possess" her.

While certainly a story of repentance and detachment from worldly reputation and possessions, Pelagia's story embodied the desert teaching on *Topos*. She made "paradise" of her cell, fully living in the present moment, trying to become like one of the angels. Desert ascetics believed that they were helping to birth God's reign on earth by their attentiveness to the Divine Presence who is everywhere.

Again we have a popular story of a woman exercising immense spiritual power while giving little thought to her reputation—she rejected fame by changing her name and living in a cave—a direct turnaround from her life as an actress living in comfort.

THAÏS

Thaïs[27] was a wealthy and beautiful courtesan living in Alexandria, Egypt. Some men sold all they had and reduced themselves to poverty in order to purchase her attention. Other foolish men came to blows over her. When the renowned desert ascetic Abba Paphnutius[28] learned of her, he came to visit her dressed in secular attire, with some coins for her time. Entering her chamber, he asked if there was still a more private chamber for their use. Yes, she replied, but only God enters this space so you're safe. Taken aback by her response, he asked why she lived this way. She acknowledged the eternal kingdom and the "future torments for sinners." "But if you know this," he asked, "why are you causing the loss of so many souls so that you will be condemned as well?"

The truth of his words pierced her heart to repentance. She asked him to meet her at a designated place in three hours, and she would leave with him and embrace whatever penance he assigned her. In those three hours, Thaïs gathered all her possessions and brought them to a public square where she set fire to all she owned, proclaiming, "Come here, all you who sinned with me, and see how I am burning whatever you gave me."

Thaïs met Abba Paphnutius and they traveled into the desert to a community of women. He led her to a small cell and sealed it closed with lead, leaving only a window so food could be passed to her. He instructed her to turn toward the east (from where early Christians expected Jesus to return at his final coming) and repeat the words "You who made me, have mercy upon me."

Three years later, concerned about what he had done, he went to see Abba Anthony to ask him if her sins had been forgiven. Abba Anthony called the community together, and they agreed to keep vigil all night long in anticipation that God might reveal to one of them whether Thaïs's sins had been forgiven. A monk received a vision in the night showing that she had been forgiven and was spotless in God's eyes.

Abba Paphnutius went to Thaïs and told her that she had been forgiven. He explained that it was not her penances that gained her salvation but her remembrance of her sins in her soul. He led her from her sealed cell and, after living among the other ammas for fifteen days, she passed away in peace.

Why Was This Story Preserved and Shared?

For a people who struggled with the fierce debates over whether there is forgiveness for sins committed after baptism, and whether there were sins that God would not or could not forgive, the story of Thaïs gave them a clear answer. There is no sin that is so great that God's mercy cannot extend there. We also love our heroes. A woman who turned from independence and wealth in pursuit "of the one true treasure" (see Matt 6:21), even to the point of burning her possessions, Thaïs was a hero.

The story of Thaïs, like other stories of forgiveness from the desert, also affirmed that forgiveness of sin is pure gift and not earned. She simply needed to be willing to accept this gift. While the idea of sealing someone in a cell appears harsh to our modern ears, it was not so to hearers in the early Christian movement. Like other ascetics, her time in the "tomb" revealed her inner strength.

EPILOGUE

The Gift of the Desert

My journey with the ammas has been a wonderfully enriching experience. In my pursuit of their stories, they have taught me by word and example. Some of my experiences began to make sense to me. The quiet pull toward change in the present has become clearer. How I want to live in the future is much more focused and understandable. They can be guides for us all.

We are a generation of seekers. We desire to know an authentic God. We want our faith to help us understand moral and ethical choices in work, education, economics, politics, and even our families. We want to integrate spirituality into every facet of our daily lives. We are questing for voices that have never been heard before. We are reclaiming women's spirituality and listening to the voices of nondominant cultures to help us find our way.

We are a generation of questioners. We do not want to be told what to do, what to think, or what to believe. We insist on figuring it out ourselves. Faith must make sense and seem logical. It must stand up to our challenges. We want to encounter God, not merely learn about God. Our spirituality must be grounded in this perpetual search.

We are a generation that yearns for wisdom figures, heroes and heroines, ammas and abbas who will show us the way. While maintaining fierce independence, we desire interdependence and community. We want our lives to have depth of meaning and purpose. We want to be connected. We secretly want someone to challenge us toward the transcendent.

While being questioners and questers, we are often lost. We follow too many fads and fashions in our search. Too often we are left with a shallow and narcissistic inner life.

The ammas show us how to begin the spiritual journey and what the elements of a life-giving and challenging spirituality are. They model healthy mentoring for us, showing us signs of what a modern amma or abba might look like.

HUMILITY

The ammas taught that humility was foundational to any serious journey into spirituality. Humility is knowing who we are and who we are not. It is about getting really real before God and others. It is foundational to self-awareness and self-knowledge, essential to a deepening spirituality. Ascetics understood that there is no authentic spirituality without humility. We would be slipping into narcissism without humility. Our desert experiences offer us the opportunity to strip away illusions and encounter the truth of who we are before God—to embrace our goodness and our weaknesses.

With humility we are open to learning, to find a better path forward. As we embrace the self that God created, we discover aspects of God's will for our lives. We are each created with gifts and talents, many yet to be discovered. In a stance of humility our life unfolds in a way that is an adventure. We are nudged and encouraged to try new experiences and discover talents we did not know we had. Of course, we sometimes come into limitations but accept them as part of our humanity, not something of which to be ashamed.

We each have limitations. If we can accept the gifts and talents breathed into us at conception and to accept that there are many talents we do not possess, we are able to live with inner freedom. In that freedom, we can cultivate the gifts we do have. While our stories from the desert ascetics tend to focus on deepening in self-knowledge and self-awareness, we also know that they were quite literate. They copied manuscripts and spent hours reading them. Ascetic communities, especially of women, also tended to educate the children in nearby villages. They exercised their talents for the benefit of others. All this they did in a stance of humility.

Humility is the fruit of letting go of all the interior stuff that weighs us down, distracts us from our life's passions and goals, and keeps us from a simple and empowering relationship with God. Humility leads to intimacy with God. This is why ascetics considered humility so important. We cannot draw close to God when we are bound up in pride (or it's inverse, low self-esteem) and insist we know it all. Rather than diminishing ego, humility brings forth a healthy ego strength that empowers us to do God's will.

Along with humility the ammas taught about the very necessity of discernment. Their daily life was about discernment: how was God calling them. This was more than about deepening their relationship with God; discernment led them to know what words to share with a seeker and how to care for their students. As theological trouble brewed, they sought to understand how they should respond to letters through discernment. At times, their actions led powerful leaders to drive them from their homes.

Knowing our deepest desires is to know something of God. God breathed these desires into us, and discerning true and false desires let ascetics know something of God's will for them. I struggled to trust that my deepest desires were God's will for me, and yet when I stepped out in trust and faith, God let me know. I did not know I had a writer in me, I did not know I had some capacity as a spiritual director, but I knew I had a passion for teaching. These now occupy a large part of my day. But to get there I had to let the Holy Spirit heal areas of low self-esteem so that, in humility, I could risk my dreams and desires. Even failures became learning experiences.

WHAT CAPTIVATES OUR HEARTS?

The ammas showed me that my life was too fast-paced and cluttered. I was trying to do too much. I found it difficult to say no to others and was always overcommitted. I was losing sight of what was important to me and never thought to prioritize my time and commitments according to my own values and interests. I had never realized that God would and could invite me to let go of everything—literally everything—that was a barrier to my own goals and to God's call in my life. The ammas began to show me the way toward an interior simplicity and detachment. They gave me permission to let go of all those things that can weigh me down and make life more difficult and cumbersome. I began to let go—one by one—all my worries, concerns, attempts to please others, and past hurtful memories. I became less burdened and more lighthearted.

The ammas teach us about the freedom that comes with detachment. "Attachment" is placing distorted importance on relationships, material goods, a successful career, or reputation. While these things are not bad in themselves, they can weigh us down and make life far too complex and difficult. We can easily confuse our truest self, our be-ing, with one of these externals. Until we have the inner vision of the true possibilities of freedom, it is hard work to let go of all that we think we need to grasp, of all that holds and possesses our hearts. It is hard work simply to discover what it is that possesses our hearts. It takes deep trust to let go of attitudes and beliefs that we once held dear. There is deep risk in change and transformation. The risk is in trusting the process of our inner journey.

How might we best recognize those things, people, and attitudes that possess our hearts and keep us from freedom?

What helps each of us move deeper toward freedom? This might be time spent with a spiritual director or counselor, simplifying our life, seeking healing and reconciliation in relationships, and continuing our growth in self-awareness. Where is strength needed? What parts of us yearn to be satisfied by God? Where are we feeding substitutes to the yearning for God? The ammas invite us to gaze inward and reflect: Are we able to "hold" our surroundings nonpossessively and in freedom, so we are not distracted?

While God always remains present to us, we can move through life oblivious to the divine presence in our midst. The ammas teach us of the importance of cultivating attentiveness to the Divine. This is mindfulness, awareness, and alertness to the many ways God and the Holy Spirit move in our life and in this world. With attentiveness, we listen deeply within, filtering out all that blocks our God-awareness. We let go of resentment, bitterness, jealousy, envy, and anxiety. We are intentionally present to each moment. We discern all that is happening in our life with a wise mentor: Is it noisy chatter, conflicting interests, or is it God whispering? God continuously invites and entices us inward toward the Divine. A wise mentor helps us to become familiar with and trust how God chooses to speak to each of us. How do we best cultivate a quiet inner spirit? Do we attend to what feeds and expands our soul? What helps us focus on God? Where is our sacred space? Have we made a cell in our home, at the ocean, or in our favorite park? It is that place where we are away and alone.

Our dominant culture tends to favor *doing* over *being*. In our frantic *doing*, our inner world can be neglected and left unheard. Our self-image and sense of self-worth are intimately connected with all our *doing*—even the *doing* of our play! We experience a measure of success in our attempts at avoiding pain, loss, and defeat. The desert invites us to face and befriend them. The desert teaches us to dwell faithfully and fruitfully in these periods of stripping and loss. We learn to live through our times of pain and sorrow, passing through the varied landscapes of our inner desert. We may feel lost, but the Divine is always with us on our sojourn, nurturing us and abiding with us.

The ammas understood that we must order our lives to support this inner journey. We need to live simply, in harmony with our surroundings. Our inner and outer worlds must be balanced. We must risk trusting our emerging relationship with God. Our signals are internal and external, physical and emotional. Are we aware of the signals that warn us that we are out of balance? Do we trust our emotions and the wisdom they express? In what ways do we cultivate listening? How do we create and protect our sacred inner space?

The ammas taught me that the way out of the frenzied pace of our culture involves both external and internal journeys. I simplified possessions and needs. I am committed to owning less, not accumulating more. I let go of all commitments and activities that did not support or fit in with my life goals. Friendships are fewer but deeper and richer. Do we give ourselves permission to say no—to self and others? Do we live intentionally, making choices by our values and goals? Do we give away everything we haven't used in the last six months?

I began literally to slow down. I am learning to be more mindful of what I am doing while I am doing it. I am not so scattered, with my mind drifting in so many directions. I am deepening the awareness of God's presence throughout my day. I stop to breathe, take note of where I am and what I am doing, and notice the Holy Spirit amid my *doing*.

MODERN-DAY IDOLS

Our world is rampant with idolatry. Accumulation of money, cars, computers and other electronic devices, allegedly famous people, careers, success, political movements, and religious leaders own our hearts—rather than God. Idols are everything to which we are deeply attached, that take the place that belongs solely to God. These idols are our known and unknown replacements for God. We create them to control our world or to attempt to define and control God. The ammas understood that the desert demanded that our idols come crashing down, teaching us that this process of stripping and detachment is the work of the desert journey. Faithfulness to this process moves us into profound and life-giving freedom.

This stripping reveals that perceptions of ourselves, others, and God are false. The ways that things are "supposed to be" aren't. The call to change does not seem optional. God no longer cooperates with all our *shoulds* and *oughts*. The God we created in our childhood no longer works. God can seem distant and even absent, silent, and cold amid our anguish. The Divine breaks free of the limited and rather legalistic expectations of who God is supposed to be for us. Instead, God beckons us toward a new way of relating with and new understandings of the Divine. We encounter God as God truly is.

Desert evokes a sense of silence and solitude, magnifying our feelings of dependence and vulnerability. With all its intensity, only the present moment exists. Our *inner desert* is the place of encounter with ourselves and God, not escape. It is in our own inner desert that our deepest self comes radically face-to-face with the Divine. Here we are invited into the transforming and consuming love of our Beloved. Our inner desert is the place of ongoing interior transformation, where we wrestle with our idols and false self. The ammas understood that the desert is where we deepen in freedom, simplicity, and compassion. Here we confront the deepest truths of our selves. The result is purity of heart.

I was being called to a deepening awareness of idols that left me unfulfilled. These frustrated my desire to draw close to God. I came to understand that God did not want to be placed into a box. God does not want to be tamed, controlled, or pasteurized. What are our signals that we are filling that space that belongs to God alone with something else? What is this tendency to accept substitutes saying about our need for God? How do we listen to our overindulgence? What helps us to have a healthy relationship with the gifts of life — ours to enjoy? What do we need to stay faithful to the long journey?

YEARNING FOR HOLINESS

The yearning for holiness remains alive today. We live with a sense that we can be more than we are. We feel the pull of the transcendent and live with a call to be the person God intended. The ammas understood that holiness was founded upon wholeness. They teach us that we must shed our false self and allow our true self to emerge. This journey toward holiness takes us deep into our inner desert. The desert is too hot a place in which to carry our emotional and spiritual excess baggage, so we begin to let go rather than continue carrying this burden. Our desert begins to remove the excess we did not know was there.

We risk shattering our false self-image, not knowing who will emerge. Over the years, we have invested much in our public persona: the self we developed during our teens and young adult years that reflects our own hopes of who we wanted to become. This is the self that developed from the expectations of others, the self that got confused with our "roles."

To discover the truest parts of ourself is risky. Our old false self is inadequate but safe because it is comfortable and familiar. Familiar pain can seem the preferred choice over an unknown that might possibly contain pain. This inward journey into the unknown requires that we let go of our old security blankets and props. We risk that our *being* is sufficient for the journey and for the encounter with our future.

In their brutal self-honesty and intentional stripping of illusion, the ammas remind us of our tendency to project our psychological issues onto others. This projection occurs when we find something emotionally unacceptable in us that we reject and attribute to others. When the mannerisms and behavior of another irritate us, this is often a signal that we do not want to face that same behavior within ourselves. Projection is part of the false self. We diminish our God-given empowerment when we spend energy projecting rather than feeding our interior life. Living from our false self drains us of our desire for self-awareness and growth. Our self-respect is undermined and our tendencies toward internalized self-hatred are fed. Where do we do a reality check around possible projections? How do we cultivate self-awareness around our projections? Do we listen for internal signals?

While the ammas could be tough, they were also compassionate. They understood that the evil one often came in the form of an inner critic. This spirit of criticism, this internalized self-hatred, takes our eyes off God and turns our gaze toward self. We would be wise to be attentive to where the *shoulds*, *oughts*, and our own sense of unworthiness drive us. What is the quality of our interior movement as we experience our lived asceticism? Is there a movement toward life and strength, or is our asceticism oppressive and draining us of life?

CONTEMPORARY ASCETICISM

The ammas taught me to rethink asceticism. I shied away from what I mistakenly thought were the ascetical practices valued in Christianity. I came to see that God hands us our daily asceticism, if only we listen. Today, my ascetical practices center on a heavy schedule of meetings: Am I centered, grounded, and ready to listen deeply? Do I prepare and come ready to share? And am I mindful and present to others?

Choices around healthy eating and exercise, giving time to someone in need, turning off our electronic devices, being truly present to family members, and choosing to do without more possessions are all contemporary ascetical practices. Discerning with a wise guide is important today. We must be careful not to overcommit, even with the best of intentions. In what small ways might we practice daily self-denial? What forms of asceticism might help to nurture spiritual maturity and develop inner strength? Are we willing to set aside our own agendas? Will we let go of our controlling tendencies? What are some of our internal signals that we are out of balance: too harsh an asceticism or too much self-indulgence?

We yearn to pray, to connect authentically with the Divine. Embarking on the path of the ammas often begins with our sense of dissatisfaction with prayer as we have known it in the past. Our prayer, which had been dormant or unsatisfying, changes. We begin to discard our old ways and go in search of new ways of communicating with God. Our prayer matures and takes on new forms. Centering prayer, *lectio divina*, Christian meditation, Taizé, and the Divine Office are all sought. Prayer moves toward the simple; often sitting silently before the Divine — in contemplative or centering prayer — is all we feel drawn to do.

We care deeply about our inner journey. Spirituality is important and many of us seek to integrate spirituality into our daily lives. We are trying to make sense of religious doctrine, ethics, and spirituality. Symbols and metaphors are a rich source for expressing our yearning for meaning. The ammas teach us to make this journey of self-discovery with a wise guide and within our community of family, friends, and kindred spirits. Within the context of this community, we discern and discover God's call in our life. We seek a life of meaning, not a series of meaningless experiences.

Today, alternative forms of faith community are springing up. Within parishes we find smaller faith-sharing communities and groups dedicated to social justice. Mixed monastic communities are developing. These are communities of married, single, and traditionally vowed members, sharing a common life of prayer and service. We continue to have desert dwellers in our midst—some are living invisible lives in the city and some are residing in primitive shelters in mountains and deserts.

Many of us yearn to slow down. Too many of us have never learned the gift of cultivating times of silence in our lives; some do not know how to return there. The ammas affirm the importance of silence and the gift silence presents. They invite us to enter into its richness and to hear the whisperings of the Holy Spirit dwelling there. Our society is bombarded with noise and distraction. We are on information overload. We can hardly hear ourselves think and are often out of touch with our feelings and values due to the senseless noise. How do we cultivate and protect our thirst for silence? Can we listen to our yearning for silence, to honor and protect it?

In this silence, the ammas teach us the art of listening, of listening from deep within our gut. We literally place ourselves into the life of the one with whom we are listening, while also listening for how God might be speaking to this situation, need, or yearning. In this listening, we are aware of our internal tapes, messages, fears, and aspirations, yet we are listening underneath this clatter for God. How do we cultivate a listening heart? How do we put ourselves in conversation with those who are different, with the oppressed and marginalized who are routinely silenced? Will we risk listening to those parts of ourselves that are messy and imperfect?

We are the sandwich generation, with young children and aging, frail parents needing our attention and support. There can be a temptation to work faster and harder, thinking that this is how we can care for two different generations with differing needs. I have learned to let go of my tendency to worry and fret. I now trust—and this has been confirmed repeatedly with experience—that the answers to these needs will emerge. There is an abundance of time and wisdom, not a scarcity. We, however, can be so frantically busy running ourselves into a nervous breakdown that we do not stop and discern God's call and wisdom in our family concerns.

We live in a noisy culture. We are constantly bombarded with information, news, music, and the ever-present advertising reminding us of all the things we do not possess. We live with the "more is better" syndrome. This leaves many of us unaware of our inner worlds, where our true desires and passions reside. Too many of us are not aware that we are burdened with internal and external clutter. How do we feed the monk and hermit within? How do we cultivate the deep cloister within, that sacred space where only God may enter? How do we most effectively quiet all the internal noise and clutter? What need for God is the noise covering up?

Our fast-paced culture is stress-producing. Pressures come at us from every side. We are exhausted from trying to keep up with all that we believe we must do. We are perfectionists trying to meet and exceed our high expectations. Do we listen to what stress might be saying to us? Are we willing to disengage? In our listening, are we willing to invite new possibilities into our lives and change? What do we do with the distractions and disruptions we experience? How do we need to respond—in self-care and prayer—to avoid despair and apathy? With whom do we discern these experiences? What inner wounds drive us from a connection to the intuition and wisdom of God within?

COMPASSION

To experience the compassion of another is a powerful experience. Compassion has the power to heal, reconcile, and give hope. The ammas teach us of the gentle strength of compassion. Compassion is the divine attribute of cherishing and reverencing the sacredness of life in a way that directly affects how we relate to others, God, all creation, and ourselves. God has revealed to us a merciful compassion that is a womb covenant, a compassion that is generative, life giving, and enabling of restoration. God's compassion is more than comforting; it is protective and creative.

This compassion requires a tenderness of heart grounded in strength. The ammas teach us of the capacity to be moved deeply by another's pain and a willingness to show them the way out without interfering with the movement of the Holy Spirit. They had a profound awareness of their place in the mystical body of Christ and that the pain of one is the pain of all. This calls forth the courage to risk being vulnerable and to risk being deeply changed and transformed by a compassionate encounter with another.

Compassion is the strength and wisdom we need in order to dwell in the midst of famine, war, greed, and misuse of power. Compassion empowers us to embrace hope and keep at the task of justice making. Compassion helps us balance our call to attend to the inner journey, to grow in holiness and yet keep asking the hard questions that move us toward a just world. Are we cultivating a compassionate stance? Do we allow our compassionate heart to emerge? Are we willing to see Christ in all and treat them accordingly? Do we extend compassion to self in order to be able to extend this to others?

PROPHETIC FREEDOM

The ammas teach us to take charge of our own lives and not to be defined by cultural expectation. In Christ we have the freedom to risk all in order to follow the lead of the Holy Spirit in preaching the good news. We are free to step away from our own cultural trappings that might keep us in bondage to our false self. The ammas' strong sense of self calls us to choose our mentors well, and then to be receptive to their teaching.

We still live under subtle and subversive pressures that undermine our sense of self-worth and hinder our following of God's call in our lives. Many of us have experienced limitations due to gender, race, religion, social, and economic background. The ammas rejected restrictive cultural roles for women, especially those that hindered pursuit of the inner journey and kept women trapped. The ammas model for us possible ways out of this trap and into a path of freedom. We need to examine our tendencies toward negative self-talk and self-limitation with a wise mentor. Where is the call in our life to risk societal expectations and norms to follow our dreams? What do we do with invitations to risk? What nurtures and supports our risk taking? How might we creatively engage our "stronger enemies"? Are we mindful of the gift to us in these difficult encounters?

Many of us struggle today with the institutional church. We love the church, the people of God, yet are too aware of its imperfections. We want our church and its leaders to be holy and Christlike. We can be frustrated in our attempts at giving voice to this hope and desire; we may not know even where to begin. The ammas spoke frankly, openly, and boldly in challenging the impious or overbearing behavior of secular and religious leaders. They listened to the yearnings and aspirations of believers and showed them the way to a deepened relationship with God. The ammas discerned and proclaimed the signs of their times. They were committed to their call. Do we exercise the prophetic voice given us, as the Spirit leads? How do we seek reconciliation between spirituality and the institutional church? How do we respond to the prophet in our midst? How do we cooperate with the church's constant call to reform?

Galatians 3:28 ("There is no such thing as Jew and Greek, slave and free, male and female, for all are one in Christ") still calls out to us today. The ammas tried to embody this fully. The challenge remains with us. Are we open to listen to and journey with peoples of differing experiences and cultures? Do we journey with the ravaged church in the barrios and ghettos? Do we welcome women and people of color into real leadership? Are there still the privileged few in our lives?

The ammas model for us a way to engage the concerns and pain of our world. Christianity is still wracked with racism, anti-Semitism, poverty and greed, misuse of power, and the marginalization of peoples. Yet there is a yearning for reconciliation, for a way to be found for Christianity to become fully one in Christ. The ammas teach us that this prophetic transformation begins with our own interior transformation, and then show us how to live out of that integrity. How do we let our spirituality influence our choices? How do we receive people of other faiths, differing cultures, and races *as Christ*? How do we let people who are different from ourselves influence, inform, and teach us? Do we allow religious differences to divide us?

SEXUALITY AND SPIRITUALITY

The ammas lived in a world with understandings of sexuality that are different from ours today. We now understand that mind and heart, sexuality and rational thought, linear thinking and heart feelings are compatible and need to be integrated as we move toward wholeness and unity with God. It is to the extent that we know ourselves that we know God: God has chosen to reveal the divine Self in this manner.

And yet we live in a world that has and continues to abuse the gift of sexuality. Misogyny,[1] the hatred of women for simply being women, has long afflicted the Christian community; and women can be just as guilty of this as men. Are we aware of this tendency within ourselves, and within our community?

Are we complicit? Might we allow women, and women allow themselves, to accept the fullness of our humanity, including our sexuality? The ammas knew of this misogyny but claimed their spiritual authority over against a society that demeaned them.

We have grown up in a world where sex has been objectified as a commodity, where we hold especially women to a standard of "beauty" that is unrealistic and is used to sell us products we do not actually need. We have commodified sex to the point that pornography no longer shocks us, and we traffic in children and women for the "sex trade." This harms the victim as well as the "customer." It is soul-damaging to victims of sex trafficking, and especially so to minors who have been violated. This was a reality of which the desert ascetics were aware, and a reality from which they disengaged. They did so by taking their slaves with them and setting them free, of communities of ascetics welcoming orphans into their midst to educate and protect them, and of deacons working with the dispossessed including orphans. We have need for tremendous healing in this area of the human community today. Might we call out pornography for what it is? Might we boycott products sold through objectified sex? Might we work with anti-trafficking groups and support those who have been called to that ministry? We need to examine our relationship to our increasingly pornographic culture and ask ourselves how we can become a healing presence.

Sexuality and spirituality are flip sides of the same coin. Sexuality expresses spirituality; spirituality expresses sexuality. Both express our longing and yearning for the Divine. Thus, abusing sexuality is to abuse spirituality and our capacity to open up to the Divine. How do we grow in awareness of our passions? In which of our passions are we not yet free? How do we honor the God who reveals Self in our sexuality, our sensuousness, and our passion? Do we express our sexuality in healthy ways? How do we work to cultivate integrity of heart that is true to whom God calls each of us to be?

THE DESERT WAY

The ammas teach us not to fear the desert, rather to see the life present there as its gift. Before I had ever heard of the desert dwellers, I had entered a desert season, not understanding that I was there nor why I was there. I did not realize there was a purpose to my desert sojourn. When I encountered the ammas, they made sense of the desert in my life. Because our initial entrance can be painful and confusing, we fear it and try to escape. We can even fear our very sanity until a wise one unpacks the potential of the desert for us. The desert requires us to explore our crisis of personal meaning. The ammas show us how the work of our desert moves us through integration toward authenticity. The fruit of the desert struggle is abundant life and deep abiding joy.

For many of us, the desert is the season often called "midlife."[2] This is the time in our life when a cacophony of feelings and unknown forces seem to converge on us. We begin to experience loneliness and depression, even amid loving family and friends. Questions emerge around our life choices and values. Struggles appear endless, hope seems lost, and unfulfilled dreams stare us in the face. We seem to be continually birthing questions with stillborn answers.

We become increasingly aware of grief in our life: sometimes quietly present, at other times nearly overwhelming. We grieve broken relationships, changes in our health, unwanted transitions, and lost opportunities. The images of God that we've grown up with—and were hardly aware of—no longer work. Old understandings of our faith tradition seem stale and irrelevant. Funerals become the time of grieving for far more than the recently deceased. The ammas exhort us to sit in this desert and let it teach us. They understood that this painful stripping must be embraced in order for healing and mature joy to emerge.

This desert may initially seem barren, dull, and colorless, but eventually our perceptions start to change. The ammas teach us to sit in the desert, and soon we begin to see the sharp contrasts and the individuality of the desert landscape. The desert eventually becomes "home": the place and quality of life we come to prefer.

Our desert experience provides the space for emptiness and contrast where our values, beliefs, and passions are revealed and refined. Here we empty ourselves of our own obstacles to God. In the space of this emptiness, we encounter the enormity of God's presence, yet our heart may feel frightened and overwhelmed in the encounter.

The ammas teach us that the desert is the place where we are forced to live with our questions along with the ambiguities and paradoxes of our life. The void begins to have depth and meaning. We hear whispers of a rich yet quiet life. We begin to perceive the subtleties of our spiritual path, and we initiate an inward repatterning toward our truest self. What we believed was stillborn begins to show faint signs of life.

The desert way is a journey of hard work, perseverance, and tenacity. The ammas teach us that the desert becomes the place of a mature repentance and conversion toward transformation into true radical freedom.

The ammas recognized and respected the diversity of the call. Each of us is invited to let the ammas be our guide. We will each express this in our own unique way. Amma Syncletica told her followers,

> Not all courses are suitable for all people. Each person should have confidence in his own disposition, because for many it is profitable to live in a community. And over others it is helpful to withdraw

on their own. For just as some plants become more flourishing when they are in humid location, while others are more stable in drier conditions, so also among humans, some flourish in the higher places, while others achieve salvation in the lower places.[3]

APPENDIX I

The Ordination Rite of Deacons in the Byzantine Tradition, Reconstructed from the Texts of Seven Manuscripts

Compiled from at least seven manuscripts by Jacob Goar in 1647 and translated by John Wijngaards.[1]

COMMENTS	PRAYER AT THE ORDINATION (*CHEIROTONIA*[2]) OF A DEACONESS
All major orders are conferred in the sanctuary, in front of the altar.	*After the sacred offertory, when the doors of the sanctuary have been opened, before the Deacon starts the litany "All Saints," the woman who is to be ordained Deacon is presented to the Bishop.*

This was a public declaration that the person was elected to the diaconate.	*He proclaims the Divine Grace:* Teach me, Lord. O Lord, impart your power to this your maidservant, so that she may perform the mystery of your ministry in holiness and fill her with your grace. *Or* Divine Grace, which always heals what is infirm and makes up for what is lacking, promotes _____, this most devout Subdeacon, to be a Deacon, Let us therefore pray that the grace of the Holy Spirit may descend upon her.
The imposition of the hand is the "matter" of the sacrament of holy orders.	*And while she bows her head, the Bishop imposes his hand on her forehead, makes the sign of the cross on it three times, and prays thus:*

Appendix I

This is the ordination prayer, the "form" of the sacrament, consisting mainly in the invocation of the Holy Spirit.

Holy and Omnipotent Lord, through the birth of your only Son our God from a Virgin according to the flesh, you have sanctified woman. You grant not only to men, but also to women the grace and coming of the Holy Spirit. Please also now, Lord, look on this your maidservant and dedicate her to the task of your diaconate, and pour out into her the abundant giving of your Holy Spirit. Preserve her while she performs her ministry [*leitourgia*] according to what is pleasing to you, in the orthodox faith and irreproachable conduct. For to you is due all glory, honor and worship, Father, Son, Holy Spirit, now and always and in all ages. Amen.

Prayers for the new woman deacon is included in the intercessory litany.	*When [people] have responded, "Amen," one of the Deacons prays as follows:* Let us pray the Lord in peace. For heavenly peace and the welfare of the whole universe, let us pray the Lord. For peace in the whole world, let us pray the Lord. For our Archbishop _____, for his priesthood, help, perseverance, peace, well-being, health and the works of his hands, let us pray the Lord. For _____ the Deaconess, who has just been ordained, and for her salvation, let us pray the Lord. That the most merciful Lord may give her a sincere and faultless diaconate, let us pray the Lord. For our most devout and beloved-by-God Emperor _____, let us pray the Lord. That we may be liberated. Receive…Save….
Again, the imposition of the hand is important.	*And while the Deacon prays the intercession, the Bishop, still holding his hand imposed on the head of the woman that was ordained, prays in this manner:*

Appendix I

This is the second ordination prayer. All ordination to major holy orders have two ordination prayers.

Lord, Master, you do not reject women who dedicate themselves to you to serve your holy precincts with sacred counsel as should be done, but admit them to the order of ministers [*leitourgôn*].
Grant the gift of your Holy Spirit also to this your maidservant who wants to dedicate herself to you and perform the grace of the diaconate, as you have granted this grace to your handmaid Phoebe, whom you had elected to the work of the ministry [*leitourgia*]. Give her also, Lord, that she may persevere without guilt in your holy temple, that she may be careful in her behavior, especially in her modesty. And make your maidservant perfect, so that, when she will stand before the judgment seat of your Christ, she may receive the worthy reward for her good behavior, through the mercy and humanity of your Only Son, to whom and-so-on.

Vesting the minister with appropriate vestment is public affirmation of her new status as deacon.	*After the response "Amen," the Bishop puts the stole of the diaconate round her neck, under her [woman's] scarf, arranging the two extremities of the stole toward the front. The Deacon who stands in the ambo then says:* Remembering all the saints, and so on....
Making the woman deacon hold the chalice again confirms her as a fully ordained deacon.	*When, at the time of communion, the newly ordained has taken part of the sacred body and precious blood, the Bishop hands her the chalice. She accepts it and puts it on the holy table [altar].*

APPENDIX 2

Ordo
A Calendar of Feasts of Holy Women

It is an ancient Christian tradition to honor our heroes and favorite saints. Feast days were chosen for special celebrations and prayers. These dates were often chosen according to the date of birth or date of death of the venerated saint. Not all the women discussed in *The Forgotten Desert Mothers* have feast days that we are aware of, and some have more than one. With the passing of time, church calendars of the Eastern Church and the Western Church began to diverge, so some saints have a different feast day in the East than in the West. In recent decades, the church calendar has removed or changed feast days. Therefore, I have tended to stay with the feast day of the first millennia of Christianity.

We should remember that saints of the early church were so declared by the faithful; there was no official Vatican office that investigated and then declared someone a "saint." We still see this today. Many of our heroes are remembered in our faith communities—and appropriately called saints by the faithful. Archbishop Oscar Romero, Martin Luther King Jr., and Dorothy Day are three contemporary examples of heroes honored as saints in many faith communities.

January

3	Fracla, Posenna, and Prompta
5	Amma Syncletica
8	Domnika
10	Theosebia
12	Caesaria
14	Macrina the Elder
	Alexandra of Egypt
24	Eusebeia Hospitia (Xenia the Merciful)
26	Paula the Elder
31	Marcella

February

3	Amma Cerona
7	Mastridia of Jerusalem
9	Apollonia of Alexandria
12	Blessed Woman Marina (East)
	Febronia of Sebapte (East)
13	Photina
21	Vitalina of Artona
23	Romana of Todi
	Gorgonia of Nazianzus

March

1	Domnina
3	Amma Piamon
10	Anastasia the Patrician
13	Euphrasia the Younger
15	Matrona

April

1	Mary the Egyptian
6	Platonida of Syria
24	Elizabeth the Wonderworker

May

2   Athanasia of Constantinople

June

18   Blessed Woman Marina (West)
25   Febronia of Sebpate (West)

July

2   Monegund, Recluse of Tours
13   Amma Sarah
17   Marcellina
19   Macrina the Younger
25   Olympias

August

5   Nonna of Nanzianzus
13   Radegunde
16   Amma Triaise

September

1   Amma Theodora; Verene
10   Nymphodora, Menodora, and Metrodora
11   Amma Theodora
19   Susanna
25   Euphrosyne of Alexandria
28   Eustochium
29   Blessed Maria the Harp Player

October

2   Justina
3   Manna of Fontenet
9   Athanasia of Antioch and Egypt
    Poplia (Publia)

GLOSSARY OF SELECTED TERMS

abba. A man who is a spiritual mentor or leader, either for one or more individuals or as the head of a monastery.

accidie. The inability to be committed to the spiritual journey; a carelessness, listlessness, indifference, or laziness toward the hard interior work of conversion and transformation. It is a failure to appropriate Christian values, often revealed through passive-aggressive behavior toward others.

amma. A woman who is a spiritual mentor or leader, either for one or more individuals or as the head of a monastery.

anchoress/anchorite. A solitary, residing either in a cave or a cell. In later Christianity, an anchoress or anchorite lived in a cell that was attached (physically) to a church. In Eastern Christianity, this term is used interchangeably with *amma/abba*.

apatheia. An intense purity of passion; a passion that is singularly directed toward God. Passion, or powerful emotions, can be a creative life force that assists and supports—or distracts and distorts—on the inner journey. Evagrius Ponticus once said, "Desert apatheia has a daughter whose name is love." Apatheia deepens our capacity for love and desire for God.

Arianism. A movement within early Christianity, condemned as a heresy, that nearly split the church and the Roman Empire. Arius of Alexandria (d. 336) taught that Christ was not equal in divinity to the first person of the Trinity but was subordinate. Arius taught that Christ was "created" and that there was a time when Christ did not exist.

ascetic. A person who dedicates every aspect of her or his life to contemplation and seeking union with God. An ascetic lives an austere life and has a regular practice of fasting, prayer, self-denial, and generosity toward the poor.

basilica. Originally, the simple and spacious meeting halls, often used for political purposes, that were common in the Roman Empire. These became the first public places of worship when Christianity moved from being principally a home-centered faith to a public religion.

catechesis. Instruction and training in the way of Jesus Christ. The teaching of the good news with all its commands, demands, and graces. This term particularly applies to preparing new believers for baptism and formal reception into the church.

cell. A single room or cave, very simple, even austere, used as a place for living, work, and prayer. The cell was the place where one encountered God in solitude.

Christology. The study and explanation of who Jesus of Nazareth is: as human and as the divine Son of God. Over the centuries, many writers have attempted to explain how Jesus is fully human and fully divine.

compunction. Contrition or remorse. In the desert tradition, compunction is understood as a piercing of our heart by sorrow. This was considered healing and necessary for inner growth. In Greek, *penthos.*

conversion. A spiritual change in priorities and commitments; a spiritual revitalization and reorientation; to live with a new heart.

deacon. From the Greek *diakonos,* meaning "servant" or "helper"; an ordained office related to priesthood. For the first several centuries, there was no separate designation between women and men as deacons; both genders were called *deacon.* Only later did gender differentiation set in (*deacon* for men and *deaconess* for women).

detachment. In desert spirituality, detachment is the process of letting go of the inner attachment to material objects, personal reputation, position in society, attitudes, and emotions. With detachment, one can own possessions without being possessed by them. For example, another's behavior is no longer irritating;

one is not concerned about theft; and emotions and feelings no longer rule one's life. It is true simplicity. In Greek, *topos*.

diaspora. To be driven, as a community or ethnic group, from one's home due to political, religious, or racial strife; an identifiable group forced to live away from its homeland. For example, the Jews were driven from Jerusalem in 70 CE, monastics were driven from their monasteries during the Arian controversy, and in modern days, Jews and African Americans are considered *in diaspora*.

discernment of spirits. To test and discern religious influences upon a person, group, or idea. In Christian tradition, a wise person is sought to prayerfully listen and perceive or distinguish between evil and God's influence: *Is this of God? Would this commitment, course of action, possession, decision move me toward or away from God?* The language comes from an era that saw demonic influence acting in humanity.

Divine Office. Also called the Liturgy of the Hours, the Office consists of chanting the psalms and sections of scripture and scripture-based prayer. It originates in the biblical prayer of the Jewish synagogue. Most popular in use are the Morning and Evening Office. However, many contemplative traditions, following the example of the ascetics, pray seven times each day.

eremitic. A person who lives a life of intense solitude. Also can refer to a religious tradition within which solitaries live alone but within proximity of one another, such as the Carthusian monastics today.

eros. For ascetics, eros was the longing to share in the Divine life, to experience God to the fullest. This was a deep desire that drove them daily to deepen their capacity for God.

Eucharist. Also called holy communion, from the Greek for "to give thanks." The Eucharist is the Christian liturgical sacrament in which the church remembers, celebrates, and proclaims Jesus's life, death, and resurrection. At the Last Supper, Jesus told his followers to "do this in memory of me."

evil one. Also called Satan or the devil, meaning accuser, slanderer, adversary, and perjurer. This is Lucifer, the fallen archangel and the embodiment of total evil, totally other from God.

fear of God. Awe and respect for the immanence and yet total otherness of God. Desert spirituality realizes that we are totally and utterly dependent upon the Divine while also being drawn and attracted to a deepening relationship with God. It is being unafraid of God.

grace. God's self-gift, freely given.

hermit. A person who withdraws from society in order to live alone. A solitary.

heterodox. Unorthodox or not quite orthodox. In the christological debates, this position held that Christ was either fully divine and only "appeared" human, or that he was fully human and not quite divine as the first person of the Trinity is divine. This term, however, can also have political implications. Many movements, or even churches in particular geographical locations, were called heterodox for having women and freed slaves in positions of leadership. Scholars today are reinvestigating movements long accused of heresy or heterodoxy to uncover portions of our tradition that have been lost in political wrangling.

idolatry. The blind adoration, reverence, devotion to anything that is not God. People, things, relationships can come to so consume and possess our lives, minds, and hearts that we lose sight of God.

kenosis. The experience of facing into the most abysmal suffering, including the loss of meaning and hope that often accompanies that suffering. In the Middle Ages, the phrase "the Dark Night" would express this experience. Ascetics taught that this suffering and emptying was the natural process of letting go of all that kept them from a deeper relationship with the Divine.

laura. A naturally hewn cave that a desert dweller would adapt to become "home."

Life. A biography of an amma, abba, martyr, or saint, often commissioned by family members or religious communities. These were usually composed in a hagiographical style with the intent of converting the reader. "Facts," in our modern, scientific sense, were not of primary concern.

Logos. The Word, as in Jesus is the Word.

Manichaeism. A religious movement, popular in Roman society, based on absolute dualism expressed in a perceived conflict between good and evil, light and darkness. Matter—the human body—imprisoned spirit, light, and truth; the "elect" utilized strict asceticism to liberate the light (today we might say, "enlightenment"). Manichaeism was condemned as a heresy.

martyrium. A church shrine that houses the relics of a saint, preferably one martyred for the faith.

mausoleum. A place of burial large enough to hold many caskets, with space to walk around and even dine, like a family chapel. Mausoleums were common residences for ascetics, as they provided privacy and were a symbol of the desire to become "like angels."

monastery. A group of people gathered around a spiritual leader, sharing the common life and prayer. There is usually a degree of seclusion from the general public as well as some form of religious vows.

monk. From the Greek *monos*, meaning "one" or "solitary"; a man or woman who lives in a monastery.

monophysite. The position that Jesus of Nazareth as God Incarnate has strictly one nature, not two. In rejecting the Council of Chalcedon's position of one person in two natures, the monophysites stressed the divine nature and rejected the humanity of Jesus. They believed that Jesus just *appeared* human.

oratory. A small chapel, not a parish church, dedicated exclusively to prayer.

orthodox. Correct religious doctrine. In the christological debates, this position held that Christ was fully human and fully divine. This teaching emerged as the officially accepted position of prominent theologians and bishops that resulted in the Nicene Creed and trinitarian theology.

penthos. Ultimately, this is the gift of tears and the call to conversion. Ascetics understood this as an interior stance of grace-filled and humble self-knowledge that we have made a choice or took an action that leads us away from God.

prosoche. This is the call to pay deep attention to one's inner world and the Holy Spirit who dwells there, an intense contemplative awareness of the present moment. Deep attention demands a keen ability to listen.

repentance. A deep inner change in disposition and attitude; a movement from despair, regret, and remorse toward serenity.

rule. The code of life that regulates the common life of a community. Although these can be legal in nature, most rules, especially in their earliest forms, are spiritual documents. Rules define prayer, commitment, simplicity, and good works; they also exhort community members in pursuit of holiness and give the justification for the community's existence.

saying. An oral teaching of an amma or abba to her or his followers that has been remembered, passed on, and eventually written down.

seder. The ceremonial meal held during Passover commemorating the deliverance of the Jewish people from Egyptian captivity, the Exodus. The seder is celebrated in the home and is presided over by the female head of the family, usually the mother.

spirituality. Phil Boroughs, SJ, defines this, within the Christian context, as "the experience and the expression of the revelation of God in the Spirit of Jesus, to which the believer lovingly responds in prayer and service as an individual, as a participant in a faith community and as a member of the human family within creation."

telos. This is the call to be present to the present moment as well as a sense of "placelessness." Ascetics saw this as a process for creating a deeper capacity for intimacy with God. There is also a sense that they sought to "bring paradise" to their present reality. In a way, to incarnate God's presence here on earth.

topos. Living with detachment and also a holy discontent. Ascetics experienced times where God seemed utterly silent and their hearts ached.

Vulgate. A translation of the Bible into the vernacular Latin, the common language of the people of the Roman Empire.

NOTES

PREFACE

1. I AM THAT I AM or I WILL BE WHO I WILL BE or I WILL BE
GRACIOUS TO WHOM I WILL BE GRACIOUS is God's answer to Moses.
See Exod 3:14 and 33:19.

CHAPTER ONE: THE WORLD OF THE DESERT MOTHERS

1. See bibliography for studies that include Jo Ann
McNamara, *Sisters in Arms: Catholic Nuns through Two Millen-
nia*; Ute Eisen, *Women Officeholders in Early Christianity*; Karen
Jo Torjesen, *When Women Were Priests*; Elizabeth Schüssler
Fiorenza, *In Memory of Her*; Kathleen E. Corley, *Private Women,
Public Meals*; Mary Malone, *Women & Christianity*. Volume 1: *The
First Thousand Years*.

2. Gal 3:28, which scholars say is one of the earliest creedal
statements in Christianity.

3. See Christine Schenk, *Crispina and Her Sisters: Women
and Authority in Early Christiantiy* (Minneapolis: Fortress, 2017).

4. See Karen Jo Torjesen, *When Women Were Priests: Wom-
en's Leadership in the Early Church and the Scandal of Their Subordination in the Rise of Christianity* (New York: HarperSanFrancisco,
1993) among other sources.

5. Slaves were often freed and treated as equal members of
the community.

6. Early literature and English language translations of this
early literature tend to use *ascetic, hermit,* and *anchorite* interchangeably, different words for the same reality.

7. See Wendy Wright, "Desert Listening," *Weavings* 9, no. 3
(May–June 1994): 12.

8. *Paphnutius: Histories of the Monks of Upper Egypt and the Life of Onnophrius*, trans. Tim Vivian (Kalamazoo, MI: Cistercian Studies, 1993), 19.

9. *Paphnutius: Histories*, 20.

Chapter Two: Desert Spirituality

1. Elizabeth Bryson Bongie, trans., *The Life of Blessed Syncletica by Pseudo-Athanasius* (Toronto: Peregrina Publishing, 1995), 56, adapted.

2. Although not original to him, the terms *true self* and *false self* are often associated with Thomas Merton, a twentieth-century ascetic and Trappist monk. The true self is that part of myself revealed in Christ. It is the person I was originally created to be: my gifts, strengths, passions, interests as well as my truest capacity to love, extend compassion, and offer hospitality. The false self is the part of myself that I have created or was created in my upbringing that is not true to the person God meant for me to be. In many ways our false self is more evident than our true self. In part, this is because our true self is revealed in God's own time and usually within community.

3. Bongie, *Life of Blessed Syncletica*, 45.

4. See Walter Brueggemann, *Praying the Psalms* (Winona, WI: St. Mary's Press, 1986).

5. *Apatheia* is not *apathy*, although the words sound similar. Our contemporary understanding of apathy is more closely connected with *acedia*.

6. Author's adaptation from Arsenius 27 and 30.

7. Judaism has a long and fruitful understanding of prayer. Prayer that comes from the heart is a bodily experience. Jews do not "sit still" while in prayer; rather, a soft, rocking motion accompanies private (and at times, public) prayer.

8. *Paphnutius: Histories of the Monks of Upper Egypt and the Life of Onnophrius*, trans. Tim Vivian (Kalamazoo, MI: Cistercian Studies, 1993), 10.

9. Kenneth Leech, *Experiencing God* (San Francisco: Harper & Row, 1985), 139–40.

10. Wendy Wright, "Desert Listening," *Weavings* 9, no. 3 (May–June 1994): 10.

11. Wright, "Desert Listening," 14.

12. Wright, "Desert Listening," 11.

CHAPTER THREE: THE SAYINGS OF THE DESERT MOTHERS

1. These Sayings are known as the *Apophthegmata Patrum* or *Sayings of the Fathers*. I base the translations of the Sayings found in this chapter upon the work of Ward, Bongie, and Vivian, adjusted for American sensibilities and inclusive language. See the bibliography for more information.

2. These theological debates concerned the nature of Christ: How could Jesus of Nazareth, the Son of God, be fully human and fully divine? Various positions were condemned as heresy—and some clearly were. The debates had political implications. Bishops such as Athanasius of Alexandria were forced from their sees for taking positions contrary to those favored by the emperor. Our Trinitarian theology developed as a result of these debates.

3. These concepts, passed down in Greek, were made most famous by the desert ascetic Evagrius the Solitary (345–99 CE).

4. As in Phil 2.

5. For example, see Inbar Graiver, *Asceticism of the Mind: Forms of Attention and Self-Transformation in Late Antique Monasticism* (Toronto: PIMS, 2018), 7.

6. For example, the ladder in Jacob's dream and Gregory of Nyssa's *Life of Moses* both use this imagery. Later, the *Rule of the Master* and the *Rule of Saint Benedict* will carry this on.

7. Elizabeth Bryson Bongie, trans., *The Life of Blessed Syncletica by Pseudo-Athanasius* (Toronto: Peregrina Publishing, 1995), 10.

8. Bongie, *Life of Blessed Syncletica*, 10.

9. Evagrius Ponticus (345–99 CE), born in present-day Turkey, united the mystical theology of Origen with the rigorous asceticism of the desert tradition.

10. See Heb 12:24.

11. Ammas deeply valued their relationships, but they let go of most casual friendships as distracting to their way of life. The relationships they kept tended to be intense and lifelong.

12. Not all relationships are healthy and worth saving; some ought to be abandoned. Healthy and valuable relationships nurture and build our self-esteem, bring joy to our life, and bring forth the best in us. We are called to do the same for others. Relationships that reinforce internalized self-hatred, that leave us unhappy with who we are, or that drain us of energy need to be evaluated with a wise person in our life. The call may be to end such a relationship.

13. The Pascal Mystery refers to Jesus's torture, death, and resurrection, honored during the Triduum, the three holy days known as Holy Thursday, Good Friday, Holy Saturday, and Easter Sunday.

14. When we accept any messages that tell us we are unworthy, unable, unacceptable, somehow "wrong"—for any reason, such as our gender, culture, race, or sexual orientation—and believe them as true, we have begun to internalize self-hatred. This affects our images of God as well as how we treat ourselves, others, and the created world.

15. For a further discussion of the prophetic, see Laura Swan, *Engaging Benedict: What the Rule Can Teach Us Today* (Notre Dame, IN: Christian Classics, 2005), chap. 9.

16. Around 540 CE, Saint Benedict will complete his Rule for his monasteries.

17. Some might recognize this as a reference to one way that the Prayer of Saint Francis (d. 1226) is translated, but it's not a good translation into American English. With doubt we are open to other possibilities, to be shown a better or more effective way. With certitudes we are not open to hearing other options or possibilities.

18. The most helpful discussion of *accidie* that I have found is in Louis J. Cameli, *The Devil You Don't Know: Recognizing and Resisting Evil in Everyday Life* (Notre Dame, IN: Ave Maria Press, 2011), chap. 5.

19. *Synaxis*, more commonly used in the Eastern Orthodox tradition, refers to the regular scheduled hours for liturgical services, such as the celebration of Mass and the Liturgy of the Hours.

20. See Douglas Burton-Christie, *The Word in the Desert: Scripture and the Quest for Holiness in Early Christian Monasticism* (Oxford: Oxford University Press, 1993), 272–73.

CHAPTER FOUR: BRIGHT STARS IN THE DESERT SKY

1. E. Wallis Budge, *The Paradise of the Holy Fathers* (Seattle: St. Nectarios Press, 1978), 96.

2. Saint Athanasius lived from 296–373 CE and served as bishop from 328 CE until his death. During this time he was exiled five times due to his defense of the orthodox position over against the Arians (who rejected the full divinity/full humanity of Christ). This particular exile occurred in 355 CE.

3. Marcella was one of the early leaders of the ascetic movement of fourth-century Rome. See chap. 6.

4. This consecration most likely included baptism.

5. Letter of Jerome to Marcella as translated in Joan M. Petersen, *Handmaids of the Lord: Contemporary Descriptions of Feminine Asceticism in the First Six Christian Centuries* (Kalamazoo, MI: Cistercian Publications, 1996), 106.

6. Petersen, *Handmaids of the Lord,* 107.

7. Athanasia had the legal right to sue her husband for theft.

8. We know that John of Ephesus (507–c. 588 CE) visited Caesaria in 541 CE and that Severus lived near her in 508–11 CE.

9. Scholars do not know whether she was widowed or she left her husband, a common and acceptable practice in her day.

10. The Roman Empire was in transition, and there was still controversy over the development of the Nicene Creed and over Arianism and other heresies.

11. Father and son ruled from 253–60 CE.

12. Copies are preserved at the Great Laura at Iveron and other Orthodox monasteries. The manuscript discovered and translated by Agnes Smith Lewis in 1892 was a palimpsest: the parchment on which the Life was written was originally an ancient gospel text that had been partially erased.

13. Much like the Passion story of Jesus's trial and crucifixion, some stories of martyrs grew in detail and elaboration. The point wasn't historical accuracy, although martyrs certainly died, but to

demonstrate the spiritual power and authority over death of the martyred person.

14. Palladius, *Lausiac History* (New York: Newman Press, 1964), 138.

15. An apocryphal story mixes myth of varying origin with a grain of historical truth or blends the lives of several persons into one story. It often grows out of an active oral tradition rather than the work of a single author. See A. J. Wensinck, ed. and trans., *Legends of Eastern Saints: Chiefly from Syriac Sources* (Leyden: E. J. Brill, 1913) for her Life.

16. Origen (185–254 CE), considered Christianity's first systematic theologian, wrote extensively on mysticism and the scriptures. He produced an edition of the Hebrew scriptures, providing six translations in parallel form. Origen was head of the catechetical school in Alexandria for twenty years, then for another twenty years at the catechetical school in Caesaria (Palestine). His works significantly influenced many theologians after him.

17. I am aware that for some scholars, Origen's presence in Caesaria of Cappadocia is controversial. Origen's presence in Caesaria of Palestine is well known. Firmilian was a friend of Origen's and invited him to weather the storm there in 235 CE. See Susanna Elm, *"Virgins of God": The Making of Asceticism in Late Antiquity*, Oxford Classical Monographs Series (Oxford: Clarendon Press, 1994), 30n13.

18. The Orthodox Church and the Roman Catholic Church separated over doctrinal and political differences in the eleventh century. The Orthodox Church is the dominant Christian church of the East and Russia.

19. Palladius, *Lausiac History*, 146. Symmachus was a Jewish translator of the Hebrew scriptures into Greek. His translations date from around 200 CE.

20. Julian the Apostate was a Roman emperor who attempted to return the empire to pagan practices. Fierce persecution against Christians and Jews ensued.

21. Partial reference in R. M. Price, trans., *Cyril of Scythopolis: The Lives of the Monks of Palestine* (Kalamazoo, MI: Cistercian Publications, 1991), 256–57.

22. She is also sometimes called Mary, Maria, or Maryana. Her Life was written in 778 CE in Syriac. See Alice-Mary Talbot, ed., *Holy Women of Byzantium: Ten Saints' Lives in English Translation* (Washington, DC: Dumbarton Oaks, 1996) for a translation of her Life.

23. One Life places her in Bithynia, in northwestern Asia Minor; another Life places her in Syriac Tripoli.

24. See Sebastian Brock and Susan Ashbrook Harvey, trans., *Holy Women of the Syrian Orient* (Berkeley: University of California Press, 1987) for a translation of their Lives.

25. Doctrinal disputes were often political, as they can be today. To extend hospitality to those who resisted the popular position was deemed political subversion.

26. Brock and Harvey, *Holy Women of the Syrian Orient*, 132.

27. The life of Matrona was written in Greek by Saint Symeon the Translator. Copies exist in the Monastery of Iveron and several other monasteries. See also Khalifa Bennasser, *Gender and Sanctity in Early Byzantine Monasticism: A Study of the Phenomenon of Female Ascetics in Male Monastic Habit with a Translation of the Life of St. Matrona* (PhD diss., Rutgers University, 1984); Talbot, *Holy Women of Byzantium*.

28. Gregory of Tours wrote a biography of Monegund. See Jo Ann McNamara and John E. Halborg, ed. and trans., *Sainted Women of the Dark Ages* (Durham: Duke University Press, 1992).

29. The Bollandists tell us that Symeon Metaphrastes is credited with recording their lives in Greek and that John Moscos made record of their story in his journals.

30. See Benedicta Ward, *Harlots of the Desert: A Study of Repentance in Early Monastic Sources* (Kalamazoo, MI: Cistercian Publications, 1987), 77–78; and *Sayings of the Desert Fathers* (Kalamazoo, MI: Cistercian Publications, 1975/1984), 93–94.

31. Brock and Harvey, *Holy Women of the Syrian Orient*, 134.

32. Adulthood was defined as twelve years of age.

33. Brock and Harvey, *Holy Women of the Syrian Orient*, 137.

34. Tim Vivian, *Journeying into God: Seven Early Monastic Lives* (Minneapolis: Augsburg Fortress, 1996), 37–50.

35. See Schroeder, "Women in Anchoritic and Semi-Anchoritic Monasticism in Egypt: Rethinking the Landscape," *Church History* 83, no. 1 (March 2014): 14–15.

Chapter Five: Deaconesses of the Early Church

1. I use both terms—*deacon* and *deaconess*—depending on the contemporary usage. For example, there are references both to the deacon Phoebe and to the deaconess Olympias. How each deacon or deaconess was called by her contemporaries is the way I use the term throughout *The Forgotten Desert Mothers*.

2. This would be 643 CE by our modern calendar.

3. *See* is the term used for the geographical location of a bishop and his leadership position.

4. Kevin Madigan and Carolyn Osiek, eds., *Ordained Women in the Early Church. A Documentary History* (Baltimore: Johns Hopkins University Press, 2005), 28.

5. Madigan and Osiek, *Ordained Women*, 29.

6. Saint Hippolytus of Rome wrote the *Apostolic Constitutions* around 215–20 CE. A partial translation may be found in Elizabeth A. Clark, *Women in the Early Church* (Collegeville, MN: Liturgical Press, 1990). For a full translation, see *Didascalia Apostolorum*, trans. R. H. Connolly (Oxford: Clarendon Press, 1929), esp. chap. 6.

7. Jo Ann McNamara, *Sisters in Arms: Catholic Nuns through Two Millennia* (Cambridge, MA: Harvard University Press, 1996), 59. Obviously women were ministering at the altar and performing other sacramental duties, otherwise there was no need to discuss this.

8. Manuscripts, also called *codices*, are given titles to identify them. Some of these manuscripts include Vatican Manuscript #1872; Codex Syriacus Vaticanus #19; the Nicolai Manuscript (its text is from Gregory of Nazianzus); and the George Varus Manuscript. See John Morinus, *Commentarius de Sacris Ecclesiae Ordinationibus* (Antwerp: Kalverstraat, 1695).

9. Clark, *Women in the Early Church*, 181.

10. Today called Wadi'n Natrun or Skete. It was the desert home of many hermits and monasteries; it is situated between Cairo and Alexandria in present-day Egypt.

11. Sebastian Brock and Susan Ashbrook Harvey, trans., *Holy Women of the Syrian Orient* (Berkeley; University of California Press, 1987), 147.

12. See chap. 4.

13. Simply put, the christological debates centered around whether Jesus of Nazareth was at once fully human and fully divine; or divine but just seemed human; or human with divine attributes. Theodoret of Cyrrhus supported the Antiochene position in opposition to the Alexandrian position.

14. See Kevin Madigan and Caroly Osiek, eds., *Ordained Women in the Early Church: A Documentary History* (Baltimore: Johns Hopkins University Press, 2005), 32.

15. The lives of Cyprian and Justina were written in Greek by Saint Symeon the Translator. Both Gregory of Nazianzen and Prudentius also mention them. However, *The Martyrdom of St. Cyprian* is filled with as much legend as fact. This Cyprian is not Cyprian of Carthage, one of the church fathers.

16. Nilus of Sinai, in a treatise entitled *De Voluntaria Puapertate* (MG 79.968–1060), identifies Magna as a deaconess.

17. See Ute Eisen, *Women Officeholders in Early Christianity*, Epigraphical and Literary Studies (Collegeville, MN: Liturgical Press, 2000), 165.

18. Egeria was a fourth-century Spanish woman whose travel journal, *Pilgrimage*, survives to this day. This pilgrimage probably took place in the early 400s CE. See George E. Gingras, trans., *Egeria: Diary of a Pilgrimage* (New York: Newman Press, 1970).

19. Also known as Gregory of Nazianzus, who was named bishop of Constantinople (d. 390 CE).

20. Our knowledge of Olympias comes from an anonymous biographer and from the patriarch of Constantinople, John Chrysostom (347–407 CE). Sozomen also mentions Olympias in his *History*.

21. Clark, *Women in the Early Church*, 225.

22. Clark, *Women in the Early Church*, 225.

23. Clark, *Women in the Early Church*, 226.

24. Clark, *Women in the Early Church*, 228–29.

25. Bishop Nectarius preceded John Chrysostom as patriarch and bishop of Constantinople.

26. Clark, *Women in the Early Church*, 230.

27. Carolinne White, *Christian Friendship in the Fourth Century* (Cambridge: Cambridge University Press, 1992), 95.

28. See chap. 6.

29. White, *Christian Friendship*, 86.

30. Clark, *Women in the Early Church*, 224.

31. Clark, *Women in the Early Church*, 228.

32. White, *Christian Friendship*, 86.

33. Scholars wonder if "Procla" is "Amproukla." See Madigan and Osiek, *Ordained Women in the Early Church*, 48.

34. See Kyriaki Karidoyanes FitzGerald, *Women Deacons in the Orthodox Church: Called to Holiness and Ministry* (Brookline, MA: Holy Cross Orthodox Press, 1998), 31–32.

35. See Madigan and Osiek, *Ordained Women in the Early Church*, 88–89, and Eisen, *Women Officeholders in Early Christianity*, 179–80.

36. See chap. 7.

37. A reference to Rom 16:1–2, where Phoebe, companion of Saint Paul, delivered his letter to the Church in Rome.

38. Because of some ambiguity around surviving texts and letters, some scholars suggest Theosebia was the sister of Gregory of Nyssa. Was this because the Church was slowly moving toward mandatory celibacy for the priesthood? Yet his work *On Virginity* does not claim celibacy for himself. The debate continues.

39. See chap. 6.

40. Lampadion, a wealthy widow, was a deaconess in Macrina's community and was in charge of the choir.

CHAPTER SIX: MENTORS OF THE MONASTIC WAY

1. Elise Boulding, "Foreword," in Brother Victor-Antoine d'Avila-Latourrette, *A Monastic Year: Reflections from a Monastery* (Dallas: Taylor Publishing, 1996).

Notes

2. A rule of life defines the characteristics of their shared life, defining times for prayer, days for fasting, work to be accomplished, care for the poor and the sick, and how the members will relate to one another. Each community wrote its own rule. The cenobitic form of monasticism that most readers are familiar with are Benedictines, Cistercians, and Trappists who live under the Rule of Benedict. Each house has an elected leader (prioress, abbess, abbot).

3. Armand Villieux, trans., *Pachomian Koinonia* (vol. 1): *The Life of Saint Pachomius and His Disciples* (Kalamazoo, MI: Cistercian Publications, 1980), 49–50, 318–20. Language adjusted for inclusivity.

4. Shenoute wrote in a complex form of Coptic language rather than the more commonly used Greek. Because Shenoute continued to live for long periods away in a cave, he sent letters rather than speaking directly to the nuns.

5. This Amma Theodora is not the Amma Theodora in chap. 3.

6. Palladius (363–c. 420/430 CE), who was from Galatia, wrote the *Lausiac History*, which recorded stories of the desert ascetics he met in Egypt. Palladius consistently saw women as equal with men in capability for the struggles of the spiritual life.

7. Colluthus was martyred in the third century in Egypt.

8. Palladius, *Lausiac History*, trans. Robert Meyer, Ancient Christian Writers 34, ed. Johannes Quasten (New York: Newman Press, 1964), 141.

9. Many of Clement of Alexandria's (150–c. 215 CE) writings have survived over time, but not his writings on the prophet Amos. Neither has the manuscript written by the Unknown Ascetic survived.

10. Although from Thagaste, Augustine (354–430 CE) is known as "Augustine of Hippo" as he had been made bishop of Hippo in 395 CE. He had spent years in Rome and Milan, present-day Italy.

11. Known as Letter 211.

12. The Rule of Augustine influenced Benedict of Nursia in writing his "little rule for his monasteries." Both the Rule of Augus-

tine and the Rule of Benedict are the two most common rules shaping religious life today.

13. As was common at this time, Macrina's brothers were around thirty-five years old when they finally agreed to baptism.

14. Joan M. Petersen, *Handmaids of the Lord: Contemporary Descriptions of Feminine Asceticism in the First Six Christian Centuries* (Kalamazoo, MI: Cistercian Publications, 1996), 59–60.

15. Petersen, *Handmaids of the Lord*, 60.

16. Petersen, *Handmaids of the Lord*, 62–63.

17. Kevin Corrigan, "Saint Macrina: The Hidden Face Behind the Tradition," in Margot H. King, *On Pilgrimage: The Best of Ten Years of* Vox Benedictina (Toronto: Peregrina Publishing, 1994), 104.

18. Composed around 380 CE.

19. Petersen, *Handmaids of the Lord*, 70–71.

20. See chap. 5.

21. See the "Bethlehem" section of this chapter for more information.

22. See the "Bethlehem" section of this chapter for more information.

23. Jerome denounced her for having married twice—the earliest utterance on the subject. Jerome considered her second marriage a crime. The early Church increasingly felt that only one marriage was justified. Once there was a divorce or death, one was to remain single and focus all attentions on Christ.

24. Jerome, Letter 77.

25. Gillian Cloke, *"This Female Man of God": Women and Spiritual Power in the Patristic Age, A.D. 350–450* (London and New York: Routledge, 1995), 169.

26. Marcella had been living the monastic life for forty-two years when Jerome arrived in Rome.

27. Jerome is famous for having translated the Bible into the Vulgate, the vernacular Latin of his day. He served as personal assistant to Pope Damasus (d. 384 CE). Known as "the Irascible," his public fights (in the form of letters) with other prominent leaders and his extensive correspondence are the source of much of our knowledge of early Christian women.

28. One strong reason for Jerome's departure was that his enemies gossiped about the amount of time Jerome spent at Marcella's community. They did not slander Marcella, however.

29. See chap. 5.

30. See chap. 4, n. 16.

31. This place is known as "Saint Paul Outside the Walls," long a Benedictine monastery where Saint Paul is reputed to be buried.

32. He ruled 364–78 CE.

33. The "christological controversies" is a reference to the fiercely differing opinions around Jesus of Nazareth, namely, how could he be both human and the Son of God. Some claimed he was human, maybe "superhuman."

34. This is a pun of Palladius, one of her biographers. *Melania* is Greek for "blackness."

35. Elizabeth A. Clark, *Women in the Early Church*, Message of the Fathers of the Church (Collegeville, MN: Liturgical Press, 1990), 214.

36. Evagrius of Pontus was born in Asia Minor (present-day Turkey) in 345 CE and died in Egypt in 399 CE. He was a major theologian in the early church with his writings on ascetical theology, prayer, and the spiritual life.

37. Rufinus was born in Italy in 345 CE. Some of our significant knowledge of women in the early Church exists because of the break in his friendship with Jerome. Their attacks often took the form of public letters.

38. Paulinus, the brother of Jerome, was ordained a priest without the consent of Bishop John of Jerusalem. This schism was between the communities of Jerusalem and Bethlehem.

39. Clark, *Women in the Early Church*, 215.

40. Clark, *Women in the Early Church*, 217.

41. Clark, *Women in the Early Church*, 220.

42. Clark, *Women in the Early Church*, 165.

43. Members of the Roman aristocracy were under enormous pressure from the emperor to have children. Too many generations had few or no children at all, and the social class was disappearing. The emperor also wanted the wealth to remain in aristocratic

hands, as that was where his power lay; the middle/merchant class was inclined to revolt.

44. Around this time, Christians began to understand that continuity of the family name and family wealth belonged within the greater Christian community. The Communion of Saints was replacing the patriarchal family.

45. Peterson, *Handmaids of the Lord*, 327.

46. Valentinian was emperor of the West from 425 to 455. Eudoxia was the daughter of Emperor Theodosius of the East and Empress Eudocia.

47. In later medieval times, the lock would be located outside and the local bishop or abbot would have the key. Today, enclosed nuns have regained control over their own lives.

48. One may presume that Caesaria contributed significantly to the development of this rule, although her more famous brother bears the name as author and originator.

49. The Council of Agde in 506 CE allowed for married people to be consecrated to the diaconate as long as the couple agreed to separate.

Chapter Seven: Desert Stories with a Moral

1. I am reliant on a translation provided informally by Dr. Tim Vivian.

2. The Rule of Pachomius strictly in limited contact between men and women. The reputation of Abba Daniel allowed an exception to this rule.

3. Palladius lived in the Thebaid for seven years, most likely 405–12 CE. See Palladius, *Lausiac History*, 96–98 and Palladius of Aspuna, *The Lausiac History*. See bibliography.

4. This story most likely emerges from the monastery founded by Mary, sister of Pachomius, and part of a complex of numerous monasteries following Pachomius's rule. See chap. 6.

5. Palladius, *Lausiac History*, 97.

6. See Benedicta Ward, *Harlots of the Desert: A Study of Repentance in Early Monastic Sources* (Kalamazoo, MI: Cistercian Publications, 1987), 92–101.

7. The "Psalter" refers to the Book of Psalms in the Tanakh/Old Testament; the "Scriptures" was a reference to the remainder of the Tanakh/Old Testament and the New Testament, possibly some of the more important early letters, such as those from Ignatius of Antioch or other Church fathers and mothers. Learning to read and understand the meaning of Scripture meant that Maria was considered quite literate.

8. See Ward, *Harlots*, 89–90.

9. Ward, *Harlots*, 35–56.

10. Ward, *Harlots*, 45.

11. This cathedral was probably the Church of the Holy Sepulcher, still a major site of pilgrimage in Jerusalem.

12. Ward, *Harlots*, 47.

13. Gluttony and lust, which are two of the seven deadly sins enunciated by Evagrius Ponticus and others, were the two areas in Mary's life that gave her the most trouble.

14. The commemoration of the Last Supper and forms part of the Triduum—the three holy days, which are the high holy feast of Christianity.

15. This is a reference to the Nicene Creed, which places the historical Mary the Egyptian in the 400s CE.

16. Ward, *Harlots*, 54–55. It is a common motif among stories of saints that they even had foreknowledge of the day of their death.

17. This story was most likely shaped by John Chrysostom's (d. 407 CE) 67th Homily on the Gospel of Matthew, preached in Antioch in 390 CE, which became popular in the late fifth century. See Ward, *Harlots*, 57–75.

18. It seems this is true, even to this day. Until the twentieth century, actresses were considered "harlots"; they were assumed to be promiscuous—a double standard.

19. Sometimes translated as Jacob.

20. Heliopolis is present-day Baalbek in Lebanon. Bishop Nonnus, whose feast day is December 2, was most likely a monk from the monasteries of Tabennisi in Egypt.

21. A woman in public without her head covered was considered quite scandalous. Thus, many of our desert ammas wore a cowl that covered their hair.

22. This occurred in an era of Christianity when some leaders felt strongly that once a person converted, they would "lose their salvation with no hope of return" if they sinned after baptism. This story supports the growing awareness that there was indeed forgiveness for sin committed after baptism.

23. Ward, *Harlots*, 71.

24. See chap. 5 for her story. Early on, deaconesses were present for the baptism and anointing of women as baptism was normally by full immersion with little or no clothing worn, and the anointing with chrism was of the full body. Today, only the forehead is anointed with chrism. It would have been scandalous if men were alone with nearly naked women being immersed fully in water.

25. Catechumens are the newly baptized being taught the ways of Christian living. The word is still used today to refer to those being prepared for baptism. In early Christianity, the training was often for up to three years after baptism.

26. Church leaders, from earliest days, exhorted ascetics to not undertake severe fasts that compromised their health. This problem has remained throughout history. Some scholars refer to this phenomenon as *holy anorexia*.

27. See Ward, *Harlots*, 83–84.

28. Abba Paphnutius died after 395 CE.

Epilogue

1. The origins of misogyny lie in ancient Greek culture.

2. Midlife becomes easier when we have tools to understand the call and work of midlife. See Bibliography for studies that include Rosemarie Carfagna, *Contemplation and Midlife Crisis*; Michelle van Loon, *Becoming Sage*; Patrick Carroll, SJ, and Katherine Marie Dyckman, SNJM, *Chaos or Creation*; Richard Olson, *Midlife Journeys*; Kathleen Fischer, *Autumn Gospel*.

3. *The Life of Blessed Syncletica by Pseudo-Athanasius*, trans. Elizabeth Bryson Bongie (Eugene, OR: Wipf and Stock, 2005), 59.

APPENDIX 1: THE ORDINATION RITES OF DEACONS

1. Goar says he found them in the Royal Library, in the private collections of Francis Cardinal Barberini, Nicolai de Nicolis, the Monastery of Crypta Ferrata, Tillianus, Allatianus, Coresianus, and Saint Mark in Florence. See also www.womenpriests.org.

2. Greek for imposition of hands, the sign of ordination.

SELECTED BIBLIOGRAPHY

I have included primary and secondary sources on the lives of women for the first thousand years of the Christian movement. I have intentionally chosen to expand my list beyond the scope of this book for several reasons. The women included in this book were part of a larger movement sweeping beyond the Roman Empire. Also, many of these resources provide threads to a study of the desert mothers while also presenting information on other women of influence.

Archer, Leonie, Susan Fischler, and Maria Wyke. *Women in Ancient Societies: An Illusion of the Night.* New York: Routledge, 1994.

Bennasser, Khalifa. *Gender and Sanctity in Early Byzantine Monasticism: A Study of the Phenomenon of Female Ascetics in Male Monastic Habit with a Translation of the Life of St. Matrona.* PhD diss., Rutgers University, 1984.

Binns, John. *Ascetics and Ambassadors of Christ: The Monasteries of Palestine, 314–631.* Oxford Early Christian Studies. Oxford: Oxford University Press, 1994.

Bjerre-Aspegren, Kerstin, and Rene Kieffer. *The Male Woman: A Feminine Ideal in the Early Church.* Stockholm: Almquist & Wiksell Intl., 1990.

Bongie, Elizabeth Bryson, trans. *The Life of Blessed Syncletica by Pseudo-Athanasius.* Eugene, OR: Wipf and Stock, 2005. Previously published by Toronto: Peregrina Publishing, 1995.

Brock, Sebastian, and Susan Ashbrook Harvey, trans. *Holy Women of the Syrian Orient.* Berkeley: University of California Press, 1987.

Brooks, E. W., trans. *John of Ephesus: Lives of the Eastern Saints.* Paris: Patrologia Orientalis, 1923.

————. *The Sixth Book of the Selected Letters of Severus, Patriarch of Antioch.* The Text and Translation Society. London: William and Norgate, 1904.

Brown, Peter. *The Body and Society: Men, Women, and Sexual Renunciation in Early Christianity.* New York: Columbia University Press, 1988.

Budge, E. Wallis. *The Book of Paradise: Being the Histories and Sayings of the Monks and Ascetics of the Egyptian Desert by Palladius, Hieronymus. The Syrian Texts, according to the Recension of 'Anân-Îshô' of Beth Abhe.* 2 vols. London, 1904; Seattle: St. Nectarios Press, 1978.

————. *The Book of the Saints of the Ethiopian Church: A Translation of the Ethiopic Synaxarium.* 4 vols. Cambridge: Cambridge University Press, 1928. Reprinted Hildesheim, New York: Georg Olms, 1976.

————. *The Paradise of the Holy Fathers.* 2 vols. Seattle: St. Nectarios Press, 1978. Reprint from the 1907 edition.

————. *The Wit and Wisdom of the Desert Fathers.* London: Syriac Systematic Collection, 1934.

Burrus, Virginia. *Chastity as Autonomy: Women in the Stories of the Apocryphal Acts.* Studies in Women and Religion, vol. 23. Lewiston, NY: E. Mellen Press, 1987.

Burton-Christie, Douglas. *The Word in the Desert: Scripture and the Quest for Holiness in Early Christian Monasticism.* Oxford: Oxford University Press, 1993.

Butler, Dom Cuthbert. *The Lausiac History of Palladius, I/II: A Critical Discussion Together with Notes on Early Egyptian Monachism.* Hildesheim: Georg Olms, 1967.

Byrne, Lavinia, ed. *The Hidden Tradition: Women's Spiritual Writings Rediscovered.* New York: Crossroad, 1991.

Cameli, Louis J. *The Devil You Don't Know: Recognizing and Resisting Evil in Everyday Life.* Notre Dame, IN: Ave Maria Press, 2011.

Cameron, Averil, and Amelie Kurt, eds. *Images of Women in Antiquity: Addresses, Essays, Lectures.* Detroit: Wayne State University Press, 1983.

Cantarella, Eva. *Pandora's Daughters: The Role and Status of Women in Greek and Roman Antiquity.* Translated by Maureen B. Fant. Baltimore and London: Johns Hopkins University Press, 1987.

Carfagna, Rosemarie, OSU. *Contemplation and Midlife Crisis: Examples from Classical and Contemporary Spirituality.* Mahwah, NJ: Paulist Press, 2008.

Carroll, Patrick, and Katherine Marie Dyckman. *Chaos or Creation: Spirituality in Mid-life.* New York: Paulist Press, 1986.

Castelli, Elizabeth A. "Pseudo-Athanasius: The Life and Activity of the Holy and Blessed Teacher Syncletica." In *Ascetic Behavior in Greco-Roman Antiquity: A Sourcebook,* 265–311. Studies in Antiquity and Christianity. Minneapolis: Fortress, 1990.

Chadwick, Owen, and Vincent Wimbush. *Western Asceticism.* Philadelphia: Westminster Press, 1958.

Chin, Catherine M., and Caroline T. Schroeder, eds. *Melania: Early Christianity through the Life of One Family.* Oakland, CA: University of California Press, 2017.

Chitty, Derwas. *The Desert a City: An Introduction to the Study of Egyptian and Palestinian Monasticism under the Christian Empire.* Crestwood, NY: St. Vladimir's Seminary Press, 1966.

Christie, Douglas. *Blue Sapphire of the Mind: Notes for a Contemplative Ecology.* Oxford: Oxford University Press, 2012.

Chryssavgis, John. *In the Heart of the Desert: the Spirituality of the Desert Fathers and Mothers.* Bloomington, IN: World Wisdom, 2008.

Clark, Elizabeth A. *Ascetic Piety and Women's Faith: Essays on Late Ancient Christianity.* Studies in Women and Religion, vol. 20. Lewiston, NY: E. Mellen Press, 1986.

———. *Jerome, Chrysostom and Friends: Essays and Translations.* Studies in Women and Religion, vol. 2. Lewiston, NY: E. Mellen Press, 1979.

———. *The Life of Melania the Younger: Introduction, Translation and Commentary.* Toronto: E. Mellen Press, 1983.

Selected Bibliography

———. *Women in the Early Church*. Message of the Fathers of the Church. Collegeville, MN: Liturgical Press, 1990.

Clark, Gillian. *Women in Late Antiquity: Pagan and Christian Lifestyles*. Oxford: Clarendon Press, 1993.

Cloke, Gillian. *"This Female Man of God": Women and Spiritual Power in the Patristic Age, A.D. 350–450*. London: Routledge, 1995.

Connolly, R. H. *Didascalia Apostolorum: The Syriac Version Translated and Accompanied by the Verona Latin Fragments*. Oxford: Clarendon, 1929.

Coon, Lynda L. *Sacred Fictions: Holy Women and Hagiography in Late Antiquity*. Philadelphia: University of Pennsylvania Press, 1997.

Coon, Lynda, and Elizabeth Sommer, eds. *That Gentle Strength: Historical Perspectives on Women in Christianity*. Charlottesville: University of Virginia, 1990.

Cooper, Kate. *Band of Angels: The Forgotten World of Early Christian Women*. New York: Overlook Press, 2013.

Corley, Kathleen E. *Private Women, Public Meals: Social Conflict in the Synoptic Tradition*. Peabody, MA: Hendrickson Publishers, 1993.

Corrigan, Kevin, trans. *The Life of Saint Macrina*. Toronto: Peregrina Publishing, 1989/1987.

Davies, Stevan. *The Revolt of the Widows: The Social World of the Apocryphal Acts*. Carbondale: Southern Illinois University, 1980.

Delahaye, H. *The Legends of the Saints*. Subsidia Hagiographica, 18. Brussels, 1927, translated by D. Attwater, 1955. London and New York, 1962.

Dronke, Peter. *Women Writers of the Middle Ages: A Critical Study of Texts from Perpetua to Marguerite Porete*. Cambridge: Cambridge University Press, 1984.

Dunbar, Agnes. *A Dictionary of Saintly Women*. 2 vols. London: George Bell & Sons, 1904.

Eckenstein, Lina. *The Women of Early Christianity*. London: Faith Press, 1935.

Egeria. *Diary of a Pilgrimage*. Translated by George Gingras. Ancient Christian Writers series. New York: Newman Press, 1970.

————. *The Pilgrimage of Egeria*. A New Translation of the Itinerarium Egeriae with Introduction and Commentary by Anne McGowan and Paul Bradshaw. Collegeville, MN: Liturgical Press, 2018.

Eisen, Ute. *Women Officeholders in Early Christianity*. Epigraphical and Literary Studies. Collegeville, MN: Liturgical Press, 2000.

Elliott, Alison Goddard. *Roads to Paradise: Reading the Lives of the Early Saints*. London: University Press of New England, 1987.

Elm, Susanna. *"Virgins of God": The Making of Asceticism in Late Antiquity*. Oxford Classical Monographs Series. Oxford: Clarendon Press, 1994.

Evelyn-White, H. G. *The Monasteries of the Wadi 'N Natrun 2: The History of the Monasteries of Nitria and of Scetis*. N.p.: New York: 1932.

Fantham, Elaine, Helene Peet Foley, Natalie Boymel Kampen, Sarah B. Pomeroy, and H. Alan Shapiro. *Women in the Classical World: Image and Text*. Oxford: Oxford University Press, 1994.

Fiorenza, Elizabeth Schüssler. *In Memory of Her: A Feminist Theological Reconstruction of Christian Origins*. New York: Crossroad, 1983.

Fischer, Kathleen. *Autumn Gospel: Women in the Second Half of Life*. Mahwah, NJ: Paulist Press, 1995.

FitzGerald, Kyriaki Karidoyanes. *Women Deacons in the Orthodox Church: Called to Holiness and Ministry*. Brookline, MA: Holy Cross Orthodox Press, 1998.

Frank, Georgia. *The Memory of the Eyes: Pilgrims to Living Saints in Christian Late Antiquity*. Berkeley: University of California Press, 2000.

Gamble, Harry Y. *Books and Readers in the Early Church: A History of Early Christian Texts*. New Haven: Yale University Press, 1995.

Graiver, Inbar. *Asceticism of the Mind: Forms of Attention and Self-Transformation in Late Antique Monasticism*. Toronto: Pontifical Institute of Mediaeval Studies, 2018.

Selected Bibliography

Grant, Robert. *Gnosticism: A Sourcebook of Heretical Writings from the Early Christian Period.* New York: Harper & Row, 1961.

Griggs, C. W. *Early Egyptian Christianity from its Origins to 451 C.E.* Leiden: Brill, 1990.

Gryson, Roger. *The Ministry of Women in the Early Church.* Collegeville, MN: Liturgical Press, 1976.

Harvey, Susan Ashbrook. *Asceticism and Society in Crisis: John of Ephesus and the Lives of the Eastern Saints.* Berkeley: University of California Press, 1990.

Hickey, Anne Ewing. *Women of the Roman Aristocracy as Christian Monastics.* Ann Arbor, MI: UMI Research Press, 1987.

Hirschfeld, Yizar. *The Judean Desert Monasteries in the Byzantine Period.* New Haven: Yale University Press, 1992.

Holy Apostles Convent. *The Lives of the Saints of the Holy Land and the Sinai Desert.* Buena Vista, CO: Buena Vista, 1988.

———. *The Lives of the Spiritual Mothers.* Buena Vista, CO: Holy Apostles Convent, 1991.

Hunt, E. D. *Holy Land Pilgrimage in the Later Roman Empire, A.D. 312–460.* Oxford: Clarendon, 1982.

Irfan, Shahid. "The Martyrs of Najran: New Documents." *Subsidia Hagiographica* 49 (1971).

Isichei, Elizabeth. *A History of Christianity in Africa: From Antiquity to the Present.* Grand Rapids, MI: Eerdmans, 1995.

Kadel, Andrew. *Matrology: A Bibliography of Writings by Christian Women from the First to the Fifteenth Centuries.* New York: Continuum, 1995.

King, Margot H. *On Pilgrimage: The Best of Ten Years of* Vox Benedictina. Toronto: Peregrina Publishing, 1994.

Kraemer, Ross Shepard, ed. *Maenads, Martyrs, Matrons, Monastics: A Sourcebook on Women's Religions in the Greco-Roman World.* Philadelphia: Fortress, 1988.

Krawiec, Rebecca. "The Role of the Female Elder in Shenoute's White Monastery." In *Christianity and Monasticism in Upper Egypt,* ed. Gawdat Gabra and Hany N. Takla, 59–71. Cairo: The American University in Cairo, 2008.

———. *Shenoute and the Women of the White Monastery.* Oxford University Press, 2001.

Laeuchli, Samuel. *Power and Sexuality: The Emergence of Canon Law at the Synod of Elvira*. Philadelphia: Temple University Press, 1972.

LaPorte, Jean. *The Role of Women in Early Christianity*. Studies in Women and Religion, vol. 7. Lewiston, NY: E. Mellen, 1982.

Lesko, Barbara S. *Women's Earliest Records: From Ancient Egypt and Western Asia*. Brown University, Providence, Rhode Island: Proceedings of the Conference on Women in the Ancient Near East, November 5–7, 1987. Atlanta: Scholars Press, 1989.

Loon, Michelle van. *Becoming Sage: Cultivating Meaning, Purpose, and Spirituality in Midlife*. Chicago, IL: Moody Publishers, 2020.

Macy, Gary, William T. Ditewig, and Phyllis Zagano. *Women Deacons: Past, Present, Future*. Mahwah, NJ: Paulist Press, 2011.

Madigan, Kevin, and Carolyn Osiek, eds. and trans. *Ordained Women in the Early Church: A Documentary History*. Baltimore: Johns Hopkins University Press, 2005.

Malone, Mary T. *Women & Christianity*. Vol. 1, *The First Thousand Years*. Maryknoll, NY: Orbis Books, 2001.

McNamara, Jo Ann. *A New Song: Celibate Women in the First Three Christian Centuries*. New York: Harrington Press, 1985.

———. *Sisters in Arms: Catholic Nuns through Two Millennia*. Cambridge, MA: Harvard University Press, 1996.

McNamara, Jo Ann, and John E. Halborg, with E. Gordon Whatley, eds. and trans. *Sainted Women of the Dark Ages*. Durham: Duke University Press, 1992.

McNary-Zak, Bernadette. *Humble Aspiration: Constructing an Early Christian Ideal*. Collegeville, MN: Cistercian Publications, 2020.

O'Connell, Elisabeth R. "Transforming Monumental Landscapes in Late Antique Egypt: Monastic Dwellings in Legal Documents from Western Thebes." *Journal of Early Christian Studies* 15 (2007): 239–73.

Oden, Amy, ed. *In Her Words: Women's Writings in the History of Christian Thought*. Nashville: Abingdon, 1994.

Okholm, Dennis. *Dangerous Passions, Deadly Sins: Learning from the Psychology of Ancient Monks*. Grand Rapids, MI: Brazos, 2014.

Olson, Richard. *Midlife Journeys: A Traveler's Guide*. Cleveland: Pilgrim, 1996.

O'Neill, J. C. "The Origins of Monasticism." In *The Making of Orthodoxy: Essays in Honour of Henry Chadwick*, Rowan Williams, ed. Cambridge: Cambridge University Press, 1989.

On Pilgrimage: The Best of Ten Years of Vox Benedictina. Toronto: Peregrina Publishing, 1994.

Pachomian Koinonia. Vol. 1, *The Life of Saint Pachomius and His Disciples*, translated, with an Introduction by Armand Villieux, Monk of Mistassini. Forward by Adalbert de Vogüé, Monk of La Pierre - qui-Vire. Kalamazoo, MI: Cistercian Publications, 1980.

Palladius. *Lausiac History*. Translation and annotation by Robert Meyer. Ancient Christian Writers series, vol. 34, edited by Johannes Quasten. New York: Newman Press, 1964.

Palladius of Aspuna. *The Lausiac History*. Edited and translated by John Wortley. Collegeville, MN: Cistercian Publications, 2015.

Pantel, Pauline Schmitt, ed. *A History of Women in the West 1: From Ancient Goddesses to Christian Saints*. Translated by Pauline Schmitt Pantell and Arthur Goldhammer. Cambridge, MA: Harvard University Press, 1992.

Paphnutius. *Histories of the Monks of Upper Egypt and the Life of Onnophrius*. Translated by Tim Vivian. Kalamazoo, MI: Cistercian Publications, 1993.

Pepin, Ron, and Hugh Feiss, trans. *Saint Mary of Egypt: Three Medieval Lives in Verse*. Collegeville, MN: Cistercian Publications, 2005.

Perkins, Judith. *The Suffering Self: Pain and Narrative Representation in the Early Christian Era*. New York: Routledge, 1995.

Petersen, Joan M. *Handmaids of the Lord: Contemporary Descriptions of Feminine Asceticism in the First Six Christian Centuries*. Kalamazoo, MI: Cistercian Publications, 1996.

Price, R. M., trans. *Cyril of Scythopolis: The Lives of the Monks of Palestine*. Kalamazoo, MI: Cistercian Publications, 1991.

Rapp, Claudia. "Figures of Female Sanctity: Byzantine Edifying Manuscripts." *Dumbarton Oaks Papers* 50 (1996): 313–44.

Roberts, Alexander, and James Donaldson, eds. "The Acts of Paul and Thecla." In *The Ante-Nicene Fathers*, vol. 8, reprint. Grand Rapids: Eerdmans, 1972.

Robinson, James M., ed. *The Nag Hammadi Library in English*. San Francisco: Harper & Row, 1988.

Robinson, Thomas A. *The Early Church: An Annotated Bibliography of Literature in English*. The American Theological Library Association, No. 33. Metuchen, NJ: Scarecrow Press, 1993.

Rousseau, P. *Ascetics, Authority, and the Church in the Age of Jerome and Cassian*. Oxford: Oxford University Press, 1978.

———. "Christian Asceticism and the Early Monks." In *Early Christianity: Origins and Evolution to A.D. 600*, edited by Ian Hazlett. London: SPCK, 1991.

Ruether, Rosemary Radford, and Eleanor McLaughlin, eds. *Women of Spirit: Female Leadership in the Jewish and Christian Tradition*. New York: Simon & Schuster, 1979.

Russell, Norman, trans. *The Lives of the Desert Fathers: The Historica Monachorum in Aegypto*. Kalamazoo, MI: Cistercian Publications, 1981.

Salisbury, Joyce E. *Church Fathers, Independent Virgins*. London: Verso, 1991.

The Sayings and Stories of the Desert Fathers and Mothers, vol. 1, translated and introduced by Tim Vivian. Collegeville, MN: Liturgical Press, 2021.

Schaff, Philip, and Henry Wace, eds. "Letter to Eustochium." In *Nicene and Post-Nicene Fathers*. Second Series, vol. 6, reprint. Grand Rapids: Eerdmans, 1972.

———. "The Soul and the Resurrection." In *Nicene and Post-Nicene Fathers*. Second Series, vol. 5, reprint. Grand Rapids: Eerdmans, 1972.

Schaffer, Mary. *The Life & Regimen of the Blessed and Holy Syncletica by Pseudo-Athanasius, Part Two: A Study of the Life*. Eugene, OR: Wipf & Stock, 2005. Previously published Toronto: Peregrina, 2001.

Selected Bibliography

Schenk, Christine. *Crispina and Her Sisters: Women and Authority in Early Christiantiy.* Minneapolis: Fortress, 2017.

Schottroff, Luise. *Lydia's Impatient Sisters: A Feminist Social History of Early Christianity.* Louisville: Westminster/John Knox Press, 1995.

Schroeder, Caroline T. "Women in Anchoritic and Semi-Anchoritic Monasticism in Egypt: Rethinking the Landscape." *Church History* 83, no. 1 (March 2014): 1–17.

Schüssler Fiorenza, Elisabeth, and Hermann Häring, eds. *The Non-Ordination of Women and the Politics of Power* (Concilium 1999/3). New York: Orbis, 1999.

Silvas, Anna M. *Macrina the Younger, Philosopher of God.* Turnhout, Belgium: Brepols, 2008.

Sivan, Hagith S. "Pilgrimage, Monasticism, and the Emergence of Christian Palestine in the 4th Century." In *The Blessings of Pilgrimage*, edited by Robert Ousterhout. Urbana and Chicago: University of Illinois Press, 1990.

Smith Lewis, Agnes, ed. *Select Narratives of Holy Women [From the Syro-Antiochene as written above the Old Syriac Gospels by John the Stylite of Beth-Mari-Qanan in A.D. 778].* Studia Sinaitica 9. London: Cambridge University Press, 1900.

Stark, Rodney. *The Rise of Christianity: A Sociologist Reconsiders History.* Princeton: Princeton University Press, 1996.

Stewart, Columba. "Rethinking the History of Monasticism East and West: A Modest Tour d'Horizon." In *Prayer and Thought in Monastic Tradition: Essays in Honour of Benedicta Ward SLG*, edited by Santha Bhattacharji, Rowan Williams, and Dominic Mattos. London: Bloomsbury T&T Clark, 2014.

———. *The World of the Desert Fathers.* Oxford: SLG Press, 1986.

Talbot, Alice-Mary, ed. *Holy Women of Byzantium: Ten Saints' Lives in English Translation.* Washington, DC: Dumbarton Oaks, 1996.

Theodoret of Cyrus. *A History of the Monks of Syria.* Translated by R. M. Price. Kalamazoo, MI: Cistercian Publications, 1985.

Thurston, Bonnie Bowman. *The Widows: A Women's Ministry in the Early Church.* Philadelphia: Fortress Press, 1989.

Topping, Eva Catafygiotu. *Saints and Sisterhood: The Lives of Forty-Eight Holy Women.* Minneapolis: Light and Life Publishing, 1990.

Torjesen, Karen Jo. *When Women Were Priests: Women's Leadership in the Early Church and the Scandal of Their Subordination in the Rise of Christianity.* New York: HarperSanFrancisco, 1993.

Vivian, Tim. "Courageous Women: Three Desert Ammas—Theodora, Sarah, and Syncletica." *American Benedictine Review* 71, no. 1 (March 2020): 75–107.

———. *Journeying into God: Seven Early Monastic Lives.* Minneapolis: Augsburg Fortress, 1996.

———. "Witness to Holiness: Abba Daniel of Scetis." *Coptic Church Review* 24, nos. 1 & 2 (Spring/Summer 2003): 2–52.

Vööbus, Arthur. *The Didascalia Apostolorum in Syriac.* Vol. 408. Louvain: Corpus Scriptorum Christianorum Orientalium, 1979.

———. *History of Asceticism in the Syrian Orient.* 2 vols. Louvain: Corpus Scriptorum Christianorum Orientalium, 1958.

Waddell, Helen. *The Desert Fathers: Translations from the Latin with an Introduction.* Ann Arbor: University of Michigan Press, 1957.

Ward, Benedicta. *The Desert Christian: Sayings of the Desert Fathers.* New York: Macmillan, 1979.

———. *Harlots of the Desert: A Study of Repentance in Early Monastic Sources.* Kalamazoo, MI: Cistercian Publications, 1987.

———. *The Sayings of the Desert Fathers.* Kalamazoo, MI: Cistercian Publications, 1975/1984.

———. *The Wisdom of the Desert Fathers.* Oxford: SLG Press, 1986.

Wensinck, A. J., ed. and trans. *Legends of Eastern Saints: Chiefly from Syriac Sources.* Leyden: E. J. Brill, 1913.

Wheeler, Rachel. *Desert Daughters, Desert Sons: Rethinking the Christian Desert Tradition.* Collegeville, MN: Liturgical Press, 2020.

Selected Bibliography

White, Caroline. *Christian Friendship in the Fourth Century*. Cambridge: Cambridge University Press, 1992.

Wijngaards, John. *No Women in Holy Orders? The Women Deacons of the Early Church*. Norwich, UK: Canterbury Press, 2002.

―――. Wijngaards Institute for Catholic Research at www.womendeacons.org.

Wilfong, T. G. *Women of Jeme: Loves in a Coptic Town in Late Antique Egypt*. Ann Arbor: University of Michigan Press. 2002.

Wilson, Katharina M. *Medieval Women Writers*. Athens: University of Georgia Press, 1984.

Wilson-Kastner, Patricia, G. Ronald Kastner, Ann Millin, Rosemary Rader, and Jeremiah Reedy. *A Lost Tradition: Women Writers of the Early Church*. New York: University Press of America, 1980.

Wimbush, Vincent L. *Ascetic Behavior in Greco-Roman Antiquity: A Sourcebook*. Minneapolis: Fortress, 1990.

Witherington, Ben. *Women and the Genesis of Christianity*. Cambridge: Cambridge University Press, 1990.

―――. *Women in the Earliest Churches*. Cambridge: Cambridge University Press, 1988.

Wortley, John. *The Spiritual Meadow of John Moschus*. Kalamazoo, MI: Cistercian Publications, 1992.

Zagano, Phyllis. *Women, Icons of Christ*. Mahwah, NJ: Paulist Press, 2020.

INDEX

Index